IN PRAISE OF

GOOD IS THE NEW COOL GUIDE TO MEANINGFUL MARKETING

"Afdhel, Bobby, and Conspiracy of Love are key partners on this journey to bring our purpose to life."

—Vicky L. Free, former CMO, Global Brand Marketing adidas

"Afdhel, Bobby, and the team at Conspiracy of Love are the real deal. Smart, empathetic, strategic and seasoned; they really know how to guide an organization to imagine and realize their essential Purpose."

—Tom Herbst, former CMO, The North Face

"Conspiracy of Love are wise and trusted partners helping us to authentically navigate the space of purpose with our brands to drive business growth."

—Ciara Dilley, Senior Vice President, PepsiCo

"Every business, brand, and individual involved in the business of brands should sit up and take note."

—Paul Woolmington, CEO, Canvas Worldwide

"As we begin to enter the golden age in which brands unlock the tremendous potential of technology to do good, VC's and founders alike should treat this book as their indispensable guide to creating disruptive businesses with integrity and soul."

—David Jones, Founder and CEO, The Brandtech World

"As the world rightly moves to stakeholder capitalism, how companies lead, market, and transform their culture will require a reexamining of purpose. Good is The New Cool should be their handbook."

—Eve Rodsky, Author *FairPlay*

GOOD IS THE NEW COOL GUIDE TO

MEANINGFUL MARKETING

HOW BRANDS CAN WIN WITH CONSCIOUS CONSUMERS

AFDHEL AZIZ & BOBBY JONES

WILEY

Copyright © 2025 by Good is the New Cool Inc. All rights reserved.

Published by John Wiley & Sons, Inc., Hoboken, New Jersey.
Published simultaneously in Canada.

No part of this publication may be reproduced, stored in a retrieval system, or transmitted in any form or by any means, electronic, mechanical, photocopying, recording, scanning, or otherwise, except as permitted under Section 107 or 108 of the 1976 United States Copyright Act, without either the prior written permission of the Publisher, or authorization through payment of the appropriate per-copy fee to the Copyright Clearance Center, Inc., 222 Rosewood Drive, Danvers, MA 01923, (978) 750-8400, fax (978) 750-4470, or on the web at www.copyright.com. Requests to the Publisher for permission should be addressed to the Permissions Department, John Wiley & Sons, Inc., 111 River Street, Hoboken, NJ 07030, (201) 748-6011, fax (201) 748-6008, or online at http://www.wiley.com/go/permission.

Trademarks: Wiley and the Wiley logo are trademarks or registered trademarks of John Wiley & Sons, Inc. and/or its affiliates in the United States and other countries and may not be used without written permission. All other trademarks are the property of their respective owners. John Wiley & Sons, Inc. is not associated with any product or vendor mentioned in this book.

Limit of Liability/Disclaimer of Warranty: While the publisher and author have used their best efforts in preparing this book, they make no representations or warranties with respect to the accuracy or completeness of the contents of this book and specifically disclaim any implied warranties of merchantability or fitness for a particular purpose. No warranty may be created or extended by sales representatives or written sales materials. The advice and strategies contained herein may not be suitable for your situation. You should consult with a professional where appropriate. Further, readers should be aware that websites listed in this work may have changed or disappeared between when this work was written and when it is read. Neither the publisher nor authors shall be liable for any loss of profit or any other commercial damages, including but not limited to special, incidental, consequential, or other damages.

For general information on our other products and services or for technical support, please contact our Customer Care Department within the United States at (800) 762-2974, outside the United States at (317) 572-3993 or fax (317) 572-4002.

Wiley also publishes its books in a variety of electronic formats. Some content that appears in print may not be available in electronic formats. For more information about Wiley products, visit our web site at www.wiley.com.

Library of Congress Cataloging-in-Publication Data is Available:

ISBN 9781394281756 (Cloth)
ISBN 9781394281763 (ePub)
ISBN 9781394281770 (ePDF)

Cover Design: Wiley

SKY10093812_121924

**FOR OUR
RESPECTIVE SONS,
MILES & NURI**

Contents

Introduction	1
Why We Wrote *Good Is the New Cool*	7
Bobby's Story	13
Afdhel's Story	19
Part I: Good Is the New Cool	**23**
Chapter 1: How Good Became the New Cool	**25**
A Day in the Life of Conscious Consumers	26
Millennials and Gen Z Have New Expectations of Brands	30
2024 Millennial and Gen Z—Purpose and Consumption Statistics	31
The Disruptive Impact of Technology on Advertising	35
The Crisis of Meaningfulness in Marketing	37
Chapter 2: The New Model of Marketing	**41**
The Time Is Now	42
How to Harness the Power of Cool	45
The Architects of Cool Are on Your Side	52
The New Nonprofits	57

vii

Part II: The Seven Principles of How to Market Like You Give a Damn — 61

Chapter 3: Know Your Purpose — 63

Scooter Braun, *Founder, SB Projects* — 65

Peter McGuinness, *President, Chobani* — 75

Amy Smith, *Chief Brand Officer, TOMS* — 83

Chapter 4: Find Your Allies — 89

Jenifer Willig, *Founder, (PRODUCT)[RED]* — 91

Greg Propper, *Cofounder, Propper Daley* — 97

Dan Goldenberg, *Call of Duty Endowment, Activision Blizzard* — 105

Chapter 5: Think Citizens, Not Consumers — 111

Fernanda Romano, *Dulux* — 113

Eric Dawson, *CEO* and Christina Rose, *CMO, Rivet* — 119

Justin Parnell, *SVP Marketing and Insights, Oreo* — 123

Chapter 6: Lead with the Cool, But Bake in the Good — 131

Jason Mayden, *Chief Design Officer, Jordan Brand, Nike* — 133

Mimi Valdés, *Chief Creative Officer, i am OTHER* — 143

Jocelyn Cooper, *Cofounder, Afropunk* — 155

Chapter 7: Don't Advertise, Solve Problems   163

Elyssa Gray, *Head of Creative and Media,*   165
Citibank

Peter Koechley, *Cofounder, Upworthy*   171

Marco Vega, *Cofounder, We Believers*   183

Chapter 8: People Are the New Media   189

Kfir Gavrieli, *Cofounder, Tieks*   191

Jaha Johnson, *Manager, Common and Usher*   195

Josie Naughton, *Cofounder, Choose Love*   209

Chapter 9: Back Up the Promise with the Proof   215

Laura Probst, *Head of Social Goodness,*   217
the Honest Company

Bobby Campbell, *Manager, Lady Gaga*   227

Andy Fyfe, *Community Development, B Lab*   239

Part III: How to Get Started Today   247

Chapter 10: Dream It, Do It, Share It!   249

Our Final Thought: Think Transformational,   253
Not Transactional

Resources and Other Links   257

References   259

About the Authors   263

Acknowledgments   267

Index   269

Introduction

As we look back at this book from the vantage point of 2025, two things become clear:

We could not have predicted the speed and scale with which Brand Purpose (the catch-all term for "marketing with meaning") would become the norm for most major brands.

How the principles we espoused in the book ("Think Citizens, Not Consumers," "Solve Problems from the Everyday to the Epic") would continue to be timeless in their application, and still relevant to today.

A brief timeline: We started writing this book in 2011, which came out in October 2016. Shortly thereafter, Donald Trump was elected president, and in many ways, his rise to power was the catalyst for brands to take a stand—some with better success than others.

We've seen the good, the bad, and the ugly since then.

We saw Nike celebrate the 20th anniversary of their iconic Just Do It by highlighting athlete and activist Colin Kaepernick with the electrifying tagline "Believe in Yourself. Even if it means sacrificing everything."

We saw Pepsi incur the wrath and ridicule of the Internet with their ill-advised Kendall Jenner campaign, which took the charged imagery of civic protest and rendered it a backdrop for a feel-good soda moment.

And yes, we've seen the fallout from the Bud Light campaign when a well-organized right-wing boycott against the brand for simply partnering with a transgender activist resulted in a massive loss of sales for the brand.

We've come full circle: from brand Purpose being practiced by a handful of brands to becoming a mainstream idea with thousands of brands going on their Purpose journey—to suffering the backlash against it.

All in the space of under seven years.

There are now a myriad of awards dedicated to brand Purpose, from the Cannes Glass Lions to the D&D Impact Awards to the Fast Company Brands That Matter Awards.

This book is also responsible for our evolution into leaders in that space. Speaking about the book put us inside some of the world's biggest companies—Coca-Cola, Pepsi Co, Mondelez, Adidas—who then asked us for help navigating this new world we had foreseen.

It led to us setting up Conspiracy of Love, our Purpose consultancy, and working with over 50 brands and companies. Here's a partial list of who we worked with:

Adidas, Akamai, Alicorp, American Family Insurance, Athleta, Banana Republic, Bare, belVita, Benevity, Bimbo Bakeries USA, Bolivar, BUILD, Chips Ahoy!, Cotton On Foundation, Crate and Barrel, Crate and Barrel, Crown Royal, Diageo, GAP, GSK, Haleon, Halls, Hewlett Packard, Hotaling & Co, LG, Molson Coors, Mucinex, Natean, Nespresso, Negrita, Nexium, Nike, Off The Eaten Path, Old Navy, Oreo, PepsiCo, Project Management Institute, Ritz, Robitussin, Sara Lee, Sephora, Skittles, Sour Patch Kids, Stacy's, Starry, Sun Life, Swedish Fish, The A2 Milk Company, The Coca-Cola Company, The Laundress, Inc., Trident, and Unilever Australia.

We're proud to have helped brands such as Ritz, Sara Lee, Sour Patch Kids, Triscuit, and many others invest millions of dollars in causes such as childhood hunger, educational scholarships, and arts and culture programs, partnering them with distinguished nonprofits such as the Thurgood Marshall College Fund, Feeding America, US Hunger, and the Boys and Girls Clubs.

Purpose has also moved beyond North America—we've worked on everything from A2 Milk in Australia to Inca Kola in Peru. It's now a global movement, with brands contacting us daily to explore how to help them grow with impact.

Introduction 3

Along the way, we became a B Corp ourselves and were proud to be recognized with a Best for the World award. We're so proud of the Conspiracy of Love team, who continue to pioneer the path forward for our clients.

Good Is the New Cool has gone from this book to become a global movement: We created the GoodCon "Festivals of Good" experiences and brought together communities of leaders from brands, nonprofits, and culture creators in Los Angeles, Sydney, Melbourne, London, and New York (in association with the United Nations).

We're developing TV shows with incredible partners such as Time Studios to help showcase "Solutionaries"—entrepreneurs tackling some of the biggest problems on the planet, from food to transport to fashion, with new companies using cutting-edge science.

We're also about to launch Good Is the New Cool as a media platform, inspiring people to live climate-positive and ethical lives. Watch this space!

In some ways, the backlash against brand Purpose (whether from advertising traditionalists or from the "anti-woke" brigade) confirms how powerful it became—and how misunderstood it was.

Brand purpose was always about walking the walk, not just talking the talk (as our principle "Back Up the Promise with the Proof" suggested). It wasn't about emotionally manipulative advertising that tugged at the heartstrings—it was about helping brands find their deep areas of impact that were in line with what their customers wanted.

What's even more fulfilling is how brand Purpose has spread beyond marketing. Companies realized that communications were just the tip of the iceberg and that they had to go on a journey to evaluate every aspect of their model, from ensuring that their sourcing and supply chains were sustainable and ethical to ensuring that the diversity within their companies and teams reflected their communities.

Today, a consumer can find information on a brand or company with a few keystrokes, instantly evaluating its bona fides. We live in an age of radical transparency, with brands unable to hide anymore.

Even more validation comes in the form of the thousands of new "purpose disruptor" brands that have emerged to disrupt multiple categories with sustainability and inclusivity at their core. From Who Gives A Crap in toilet paper to Pangaia in fashion, customers now have an incredible breadth of choices when it comes to living a conscious lifestyle.

Today, it is possible for someone to go from the moment they wake up to the moment they sleep and only use products and services that are both "Good and Cool." Read "A Day in the Life of a Conscious Consumer" in the next chapter to get an idea of what we're talking about.

If you think millennials and Gen Z are passionate about supporting brands that positively impact the world, Gen Alpha (the demographic born from 2010 onward) feels the same way. According to data from GWI, 66% of them want to buy from companies with a purpose. As the most diverse generation in history, representation matters—and as the generation that will bear the brunt of climate change, they want to see swift and massive action from the companies they support.

We hope you enjoy this "remix" of our original book. We've tried to remain true to the timeless ideas we championed while updating our data, some case studies, and references to reflect the reality we live in today.

We'll leave you with one final thought: we believe meaningful marketing is more urgently needed than ever.

For instance, the rise of artificial intelligence has thrown up new ethical dilemmas that brands must navigate. Without a strong brand purpose at their core, with clear values and ideas on how to positively impact the world, it would be all too easy for brands to give in to the worst ideas with enormously damaging consequences.

If the world is to find a way to eliminate capitalism's worst excesses and evolve into a decarbonized, regenerative, inclusive model that balances the needs of people, planet, and profit, then we need marketers to lead the way.

We need marketers to "make markets" by developing innovative new products and services that help people live sustainable and ethical lives—and we need them to use the incredible power of storytelling and experiences to inspire them to go on a journey to make changes in their lives.

If we do so, we believe that we can create a world where people's consumption choices can not only help us stave off the worst effects of climate change but also raise the standard of living of billions of people around the world.

Far from brand purpose being over, we are just getting started.

So stand your ground. Don't be distracted by the rhetoric.

Your values drive your value, both as an individual and as a brand.

We can't wait to see what you do next!

Afdhel and Bobby

PS: And we'd love to hear about your work and how this book has inspired you. Please email as at purpose@conspiracyoflove.co.

Why We Wrote Good Is the New Cool

I t's a Saturday afternoon in Soho, New York. The streets are packed with shoppers and tourists, all busy exploring the luxury designer stores that are clustered in the area: Paul Smith, Prada, Balenciaga. Yet outside one store is a scene that looks more like a nightclub than a retail outlet, with a velvet rope and security guards. People are lined up outside, patiently waiting their turn, until the crush inside the store reduces enough to let them in. This isn't some high-end luxury boutique; this is a store that sells $95 eyeglasses and for every pair bought, distributes a pair to someone in need. This is Warby Parker.

Inside the store, the lucky ones who have gotten in are eagerly trying on pairs of retro-themed eyewear with names drawn from literature (Beckett, Huxley, Chandler) and Americana (Roosevelt, Marshall, Langston). The look of the store is inspired by the New York Public Library—all rolling ladders and floor-to-ceiling shelves with beautifully presented merchandise and vintage books, all of which helps to convey the inclusive yet aspirational allure of the brand.

Supercool design has been a huge factor in the success of the brand. After all, people want to look good first; regardless of any social good intent, the products themselves have to be appealing. The frames instantly give wearers the kind of bookish, hipster image one sees in the pages of *GQ* and *Vogue* (both of which have covered the brand with the kind of breathless fandom that used to be reserved for Gucci and Tom Ford).

But an equally crucial part of what drives the success of Warby Parker is that for every pair of eyeglasses bought, the equivalent cost is donated to VisionSpring, a nonprofit whose goal is to provide eye care to those in need, both by training people in developing countries to give basic eye exams and by selling affordable glasses.

Instead of a straight donation model, this creates a more sustainable approach, helping build the long-term infrastructure for eye care. To date, more than 15 million pairs of glasses have been distributed across the world. This aspect of Warby Parker is a large part of why wearing the glasses makes devotees of the brand feel so good, and it makes them want to tell others to purchase the brand. In doing so, Warby Parker has managed to create the Holy Grail for brands: a word-of-mouth magnet. A full 50% of customers coming to the website do so on the recommendation of a friend.

Warby Parker has managed to come up with something remarkable: a brand that disrupts the status quo economically (selling designer frames for $95), logistically (selling them online), stylistically (taking retro cool to the world), and socially (their impact in the developing world). In doing so, they have also created a business that in 2024 is now valued at a staggering $1.65 billion. How did they do that?

Warby Parker is the perfect example of a brand that has figured out the model for success we unveil in this book: how to "Make Money and Do Good by Harnessing the Power of Cool." They understand that today's customers want it all, and they have created a purpose-driven business all of us can learn from.

But they are far from alone in today's world. Brands such as TOMS, Tesla, Etsy, Kickstarter, Patagonia, Ben & Jerry's, and many others are also figuring out how to use this combination of "commerce, culture, and conscience" (as we call it) to create brands with passionately loyal followings. Not to mention the thousands of B Corps (or benefit corporations) out there that have embarked on a mission to upgrade business to go beyond the tired, short-term thinking of only driving shareholder value to the much more profound approach of also driving societal value.

We believe we are witnessing a seismic shift in popular culture— one where doing good has become its own form of cool, creating a unique opportunity for brands, nonprofits, and artists to learn from each other and work together. We believe this is being driven by three key factors: the new expectations of millennials and Generation Z, the crisis of meaningfulness in marketing and advertising, and the disruptive opportunities afforded by technology. In the upcoming chapters, we're going to dive deeper into all of these factors and unearth what they mean for us.

Our mission in this book is to track this profound change in the zeitgeist, and also to show you how marketing has a crucial role to play in this brave new world. Marketing is consistently ranked as one of the least valuable professions in society, but we believe this new approach could both elevate it and show how marketing can help save the world. We propose something radical: replacing the broken 20th-century approach to marketing that is fixated on advertising with an altogether new one, where "great marketing optimizes life."

Seeing this shift in business and culture, we were inspired to learn more about the pioneers that are leading this new movement, and we're going to share our journey with you. We're going to meet men and women from all backgrounds, at all stages of their careers—from the managers of some of the biggest music superstars in the world to the inspiring marketers leading brands from Oreo, Chobani, and TOMS to Citibank, Zappos, and the Honest Company, and some of the hardworking young hustlers and entrepreneurs who are just starting to make a dent in the worlds of business and nonprofits.

We're going to share what we've learned from their journeys in seven principles that can be used by anyone in any organization anywhere. There are lessons on how to "find your purpose" and "find your allies"; how to incorporate principles such as "treat people as citizens, not consumers" and "don't advertise, solve problems" as you design and plan; and how to execute ideas of impact by using

GREAT MARKETING OPTIMIZES LIFE

insights such as "lead with the cool," "people are the new media," and "back up the promise with the proof." All which add up to our central idea: "great marketing optimizes life."

And then, finally, we're going to give you a checklist of how you can take these things you will have learned and apply them to your day-to-day work in a way that will help you personally find more meaning in what you do, and help your organization future-proof itself for the next 100 years.

While writing this book we had an epiphany: we realized that as marketers, we no longer have to choose between quitting our day job to join a nonprofit (more meaningful but perhaps where we would have to start from the beginning again) or staying where we are, doing the same work (respected, well paid, but unfulfilled).

We hope this book shows you that there is a third option: we can do an amazing amount of good from right where we are today, in ways that grow our brands and our businesses, while also contributing to society—a much bigger win-win-win for all.

Because this book is all about people and their purposes, it may help you to know a little bit about us, the authors, and our own purposes. We couldn't have come from two more different backgrounds, but there was something we had in common that drew us to this bigger idea.

Bobby's Story

It was another late night at the office—the time of evening when most parents are tucking their kids into bed, friends are having a round of drinks, or others are maybe just sitting on their couch watching the latest addictive hit show. However, on this evening, like many others before, I was in front of a computer screen staring at a PowerPoint slide and trying to find the perfect image to add to a presentation for a morning meeting. It was December, and my mind was wandering, reflecting on the year that was quickly coming to an end.

We had had a great year—the best year ever—winning big marketing-agency-of-record accounts, helping to transform the way global clients understood youth culture, and becoming award-winning industry leaders in the process.

But as I sat in that office, I was miserable. There were perks to the job, and I worked with great people, but my life was becoming consumed by the stress of the work—seven-day workweeks, constant client demands, internal company revenue pressures, and never-ending fire drills. More and more, I found myself asking questions: *What is all this for? Does this work even matter? Where is the joy in this?* And I wasn't alone. Oftentimes, my clients were just as unhappy and stressed, dealing with all the pressures of selling more things that people were caring less about. I knew there had to be a better way; I just didn't know what it was.

In my heart, I believed I had a bigger purpose than the work I was doing, but I needed help to figure out what it was. After months of procrastination, I finally reached out to the only person I knew who could relate to the position I was in—Tru Pettigrew, my former boss, mentor, and friend. I had witnessed him go through this same stress. I called him one day and simply said I needed help. I was at my wits' end and knew he would understand. What I did not know at the time was that he had recently started his own practice to help others discover their passion and purpose, and he was testing a new model for his work. It was perfect timing! We agreed to start the process the following week, and I began it with a simple prayer: "God, please give me clarity of my purpose and the courage necessary to fulfill it." And with that, we started on a journey of discovery together.

We went through months of exploration to better understand by gifts, passions, and purpose. I wrote out my vision for my life, listed the things I valued most, and we talked weekly about my progress and what I was learning from the process; and the final exercise was to put on paper a statement of purpose detailing how I exist to serve. It was a hard exercise, a lot tougher than I would have expected. I struggled for weeks to articulate it and get it right; nothing was more important than gaining the clarity I had previously prayed for. One day in December—a year after that late night in the office—I was traveling to Washington, DC, struggling to write my statement of purpose, and I remembered a story by my friend Eric Dawson. Eric was founder of Peace First, a nonprofit organization I had always admired and for which I had served as a marketing adviser for years. The first time I met Eric, he told me a story that had inspired his work:

One evening, an elderly Cherokee brave told his grandson about a battle that goes on inside people. He said, "My son, the battle is between two 'wolves' inside us all. One is evil. It is anger, envy, jealousy, sorrow, regret, greed, arrogance, self-pity, guilt, resentment, inferiority, lies, false pride, superiority, and ego. The other is good. It is joy, peace, love, hope, serenity, humility, kindness, benevolence, empathy, generosity, truth, compassion, and faith."

The grandson thought about it for a minute and then asked his grandfather, "Which wolf wins?"

The old Cherokee simply replied, "The one that you feed."

And it hit me. That is what I've always been trying to do in my work in youth marketing: feed the good wolf. It became crystal clear at that instant that my purpose was to use my gifts and talents to feed the good in young people around the world. That moment of clarity was so powerful it literally gave me chills. Everything that had happened up to that point made so much more sense—it had all happened for a reason.

Unexpectedly, a few weeks later Eric called to catch up. He asked how I was doing, and I told him about my journey and the impact of the story he had shared with me. He could sense the excitement in my voice and the new conflict I was facing of how to fulfill this purpose as a marketer.

He told me he was at a crossroads with Peace First and wanted a partner to help take the work of his small organization and connect it with millions of young people looking to change the world for the better, as peacemakers. He wanted me to be that partner. Some months later I became the chief marketing and communications officer at Peace First, where I am now working to feed the good in millions of young people around the world.

I am sharing my story as a testimony that once you truly seek to influence a greater good, opportunities reveal themselves to do so. My opportunity and journey may be very different from yours, but I wrote this book with Afdhel because I know many of you are working in offices and coffee shops, looking for ways to do more meaningful work, but you just need to know how; and the good news is you don't have to leave your day jobs. My intent is to help fellow marketers use more of their talents and resources to influence a greater good, right where they are.

I hope this book will make a positive impact in the lives of marketers, customers, and our communities while, in the process, helping give me more courage, confidence, and credibility to serve others on a greater scale.

16 GOOD IS THE NEW COOL GUIDE TO MEANINGFUL MARKETING

THE TWO
MOST **IMPORTANT** DAYS
OF YOUR LIFE

ARE THE DAY YOU WERE
BORN
and

THE DAY YOU FIND OUT
WHY.

—MARK TWAIN

Afdhel's Story

There's a great quote from Mark Twain: "The two most important days of your life are the day you were born, and the day you find out why."

The day I found out why was the day after Christmas in 2004, when the devastating Indian Ocean tsunami struck the shores of Sri Lanka, my country of birth and where I grew up. I was there for my brother's wedding, but the occasion for joy was overshadowed by one of the biggest natural disasters the country had ever seen. By some miracle, when the wave hit, I was safe in Colombo, the capital city, out of harm's way. More than 30,000 people died on one day, a catastrophe of epic proportions. Like the rest of my friends and family, I got involved in the emergency operations to help the survivors. I can't remember much of the next few weeks; it was a blur of loading up food and medicine trucks, visiting refugee camps, and trying to cope with the sheer immensity of the horror that had struck my beautiful island home.

After the tsunami, I went back to London, where I lived at the time. I would be walking down the street and suddenly burst into tears for no apparent reason. It was only later that I was diagnosed with post-traumatic stress disorder and had to seek counseling. I was diagnosed with survivor guilt: Why had I survived when so many others hadn't? I quit my job and went traveling around the world for six months. I thought a lot about what I wanted to do with my life. I was bone-tired after working around the clock, and I had been chain-smoking two packs a day. And beneath that physical and mental exhaustion, there was something missing: there was no sense of achievement, no sense of joy at what I was doing for a living. I just felt . . . empty. It made me completely reassess what was really meaningful in life and my role in the world.

Up to that point, I had been happy in my chosen career of marketing. But after seeing the death and devastation that had hit the country of my birth, and how little I could do to help it, I started to wonder, did what I do for a living matter in the grand scheme of things? I began to feel that somehow there was something else I could do with my time and energy, something that had a deeper meaning than helping create clever marketing campaigns. I didn't want my legacy on this planet to be that I just helped persuade people to buy more stuff. I wanted to do something more meaningful with the opportunities I had been given in life.

I began to think about ways for marketing to really be innovative. Instead of trying to come up with an even glossier print ad or a more seductive TV spot, what if you could find ways to optimize customers' lives? I wondered whether this could be accomplished by creating services, products, and experiences that filled an unmet need in their lives so that instead of trying to find ways to block marketers out, they would not only appreciate the marketing but also go on to become those marketers' biggest advocates? Was there a way to drive the business and the brand in a way that was also positive for the consumer and society? That was the beginning of the journey that led to collaborating with my friend and coauthor, Bobby.

As authors, our purpose is to inspire others to join in this movement to be better marketers and citizens. In fact, we'd state our goal as simply: "To inspire 100 percent of people reading this book to do 100 percent more good in the world."

And we believe that there is a brand-new model for marketing that allows brands to "make money and do good by harnessing the power of cool," which we want to explore and unpack in this book.

So let's start by taking a look at the three biggest drivers of this shift in culture that we've observed—generational, technological, and spiritual.

Part I

Good Is the New Cool

Chapter 1

How Good Became the New Cool

A Day in the Life of Conscious Consumers

In 2016, when we cowrote this first book, the number of brands that were both good and cool were just a handful.

But today, it is possible to live in a world where everything you buy and consume is not only sustainable and socially conscious—but also cool and aspirational. Here's a snapshot of a day in the life of a fictional conscious consumer couple—Aaron and Keisha—to bring this to life.

***

Aaron wakes up at 6 a.m., snug in his Four Leaves bed linen. The alarm chimes softly on his (PRODUCT)^{RED} iPhone. He quickly turns it off before it wakes up his partner, and walks into his kitchen where the coffee machine is brewing a fresh pot of Grounds and Hounds, his favorite blend, which also supports pet adoptions. He pours himself a cup and looks at his phone. On the Tesla app, the Powerwall battery shows a full charge from the solar array on his roof, keeping his family safe from the possibility of power outages, increasingly common in Southern California.

He scrolls through Instagram while he drinks his coffee, checking out the Good Is the New Cool site for inspiration, noting a supercool Lomi home composting device that has gotten great reviews. He's been looking for a way to utilize their organic food scraps for their garden, alongside their LettuceGrow hydroponic system. He also checks out a story on greywater systems, and how they can help utilize the hundreds of gallons a day used by households to irrigate their fruits and vegetables, as well as a story on urban beehives.

He decides to do their weekly grocery shopping and logs on to his laptop. They are out of Blueland water-free laundry tablets, so he adds them to the cart, as well as Mood Tea (which raises money for mental health), his favorite Ben & Jerry's flavor (a collaboration with Chance the Rapper that supports his Socialworks nonprofit), and Moonshot crackers, a pioneering regenerative agriculture brand.

Into his cart goes Chobani's Hero Batch yogurt (supporting veterans), Hellmann's Mayonnaise (fighting food waste) Stacy's Pita Chips (supporting women-owned businesses), Boxed Water, and Triscuit (investing in solving food deserts).

He also buys a bottle of Air Co vodka (made from CO_2) as well as a bottle of La Caudrilla wine (with profits going to the farmworkers who made it) as a housewarming present for their friends. For their own house, he chooses from the One Hope Wine club with money going to their favorite breast cancer charity. And finally, he sees a notification for their Loop delivery of household goods in zero-waste packaging, arriving later today.

He gets ready to go for a run, lacing up his Adidas Parley for the Ocean sneakers made of ocean plastic, over his Bombas socks. As he runs around the neighborhood, he sees the plethora of electric cars in his neighborhood—everything from high-end Mercedes and BMWs, to more modest Volvos and Toyotas. He sees his neighbor has bought a brand new Ford F-150 Lightning electric pick-up truck and makes a mental note to ask him about the experience. He's heard it can even power a home in the case of an outage.

He gets back home and dumps his running clothes in the washing machine, using Dropp's plastic-free laundry tablets. In the shower, he uses his favorite Right to Shower gel (which supports mobile shower units for the homeless), followed by Lush shampoo bars.

He takes a look at his wardrobe, deciding what to wear today. Should it be the vintage Kenzo sweatshirt he bought on Depop?

The One Golden Thread regenerative t-shirt, his Unless Collective work shirt, or the limited edition King Owusu sweatshirt from GalerieNumber8, which specializes in up-and-coming African designers? He decides on the Naadam sustainable Mongolian cashmere sweatpants, a sweatshirt from Madhappy, a social enterprise which supports mental health, layered over a Patagonia t-shirt.

He contemplates his footwear choices: TOM's espadrilles, Rens sneakers (made of coffee), but finally decides on his Allbirds x Adidas lowest carbon footprint sneaker. He picks out his eyewear: a pair of stylish Warby Parker frames for regular glasses and Covalent carbon-negative sunglasses. He kisses his wife, Keisha, as he heads out of the door and drives to his day of meetings in his new Rivian electric pick-up.

Keisha sits down at her Chopvalue desk and powers up her Macbook Air. She's been meaning to check up on their investment portfolio for a while. She logs into Aspiration to check on their Redwood 401(k), invested in a fossil-fuel-free portfolio. She checks on their Nico REIT, invested in real estate in their local community in Echo Park, and their C-Note portfolio, which gives loans to underserved communities. Via an equity crowdfunding platform, they are also invested in Boxabl, a revolutionary start-up that is creating affordable housing that unfolds in hours. She notes that their Tulipshare activist investment fund is mounting a new campaign to persuade Coca-Cola to move to a circular economy model. And finally she checks their Lemonade home insurance, where she sees how much has been given back to their favorite charity.

She heads for her lunch meeting at the Butcher's Daughter, an ultra-hip plant-based restaurant. As she drives down the crowded street in her Polestar electric car, she sees the local Shinola store, and that reminds her that she wanted to get a watch for her dad's birthday present—she loves the brand because it's bringing jobs back to Detroit. At lunch, she eats an Impossible Burger, while her guest eats a delicious vegan zucchini and ricotta pizza.

That evening, she takes a break in her day by doing a session on her Breathwrk app, which donates a free membership to someone for every person who joins. She decides to do some online shopping. She checks out For Days, a circular fashion brand, as well as Mate, an LA-based woman-owned sustainable fashion line, and Triarchy, who make her favorite water-reduced denim. She browses The Real Real to find inspiration for cool vintage fashion, as well as Cise, who makes her favorite "Protect Black Women" handbag.

She stocks up on her personal toiletries: her Bite toothpaste, her Oui Razor, her Last Swab cotton buds. She checks out the new mascaras on Selena Gomez's Rare Beauty make-up site where 1% of the proceeds go to mental health. She buys some more of her favorite Thinx period underwear, as well as some home goods: Public Goods conditioner, Grove Collaborative dish soap, and Who Gives A Crap toilet paper, which funds sanitation projects around the world.

For their son, she checks out Thred Up to find a cool vintage AC-DC t-shirt that he's been asking for, and also buys him a Fair Harbor pair of swim shorts made from recycled plastic. She puts all her shopping either on her Aspiration Zero credit card, which plants trees with every purchase, or her Greenwood debit card, which supports Black communities.

That evening, they both relax with a glass of rose from La Fete Du Rose, a Black-owned business, and catch up with their son about each other's days while they cook from their weekly order of Seatopia sustainable aquaculture products as well as vegetables from their Imperfect foods order.

They watch the documentary *We Feed People* about Chef Jose Andreas and the amazing work of World Central Kitchen. At night, they change into their favorite Pangaia seaweed fiber pajamas, before retiring to bed.

To quote Anne Lappe, every dollar they've spent today is a vote toward the kind of world they want to live in.

Millennials and Gen Z Have New Expectations of Brands

Looking at the news headlines today, it would be easy to fall into a state of deep despair. Stories of extreme climate change, preventable diseases, economic inequality, social injustice, and the failure of our key institutions—government, banks, and corporations—dominate the news cycles and social media feeds.

Yet from traveling around the world and talking with young people, it is clear the millennial (those born between the early 1980s and the mid 1990s) and Generation Z (born between the mid 1990s and the early 2010s) generations have a real sense of optimism about the future of this planet. How can that be?

For many in the media and marketing worlds, millennials have been viewed as the "me" generation. However, for a generation that has proven to be connected and compassionate to the experiences of others around the world, a more appropriate title may be the "we" generation.

Growing up in a time when everything, including traditional values, politics, and economics, is collapsing and being redefined around them, millennials are experiencing a unique confluence of empathy and empowerment. Connected via myriad social media platforms and mobile devices, this generation has been able to see and share experiences of troubles and unrest in real time, creating a "glocal" sense of shared struggle with their peers around the world.

There is also a collective feeling by young people that these adverse conditions were created by a previous generation of adults who screwed it up for everyone. However, these young people are not playing the role of the victim; rather, they are seizing the opportunity to do something about it—to help make things better, while along the way redefining societal norms and disrupting business as usual.

Younger generations want experiences over products, sharing versus sole ownership, and entrepreneurship versus employment. And these shifts in values are for good reason: these younger generations have seen their parents' generation work themselves to the bone to—quoting finance expert Dave Ramsey—"buy things they don't need, with money they didn't have to impress people they didn't like," only to see them lose it all to financial crises and downsizing (Ramsey 2009).

2024 Millennial and Gen Z—Purpose and Consumption Statistics

Consider these statistics: millennials worldwide number around 1.8 billion (23% of the global population) and command a staggering $2.45 trillion in spending power (Khoros 2023).

And hot on the heels of millennials comes Generation Z, representing 40% of consumers worldwide with an estimated spending power of $450 billion (Snapchat 2023).

According to a 2024 Deloitte Survey (which connected with nearly 23,000 respondents across 44 countries) 3 in 10 Gen Zs (30%) and millennials (29%) conduct research on a company's environmental impact and policies before buying products or services from them (Deloite 2024).

Because of this homework, a quarter of Gen Zs (25%) and millennials (24%) said they have stopped or lessened a relationship with a business because of unsustainable practices in its supply chain.

Their consumption behavior is also changing: many avoid fast fashion, reduce air travel, eat a more plant-based or even vegan diet, or purchase electric vehicles. Keeping these trends in mind is crucial when planning the future innovation path of your business.

Here's some good news, though:

About two-thirds of Gen Zs (64%) and millennials (63%) are willing to pay more to purchase environmentally sustainable products or services. Purpose drives premiumization for your brand, and smart marketers should make sure to explore this strategy to show clear ROI.

Both of these generations have realized, to quote the writer Anna Lappé, "Every time you spend money, you're casting a vote for the type of world [you] want to live in."

But these trends don't just affect purchase decisions; for CEOs and business leaders, they have a profound impact around hiring and retaining the right talent. According to the PWC "Millennials at Work: Reshaping the Workforce" report (PwC 2012), by 2025, millennials will constitute approximately 75% of the US workforce and 50% of the global workforce.

Similarly, the Zurich Insurance Group anticipates that Gen Z will represent 27% of the workforce by 2025 (Zurich 2022). In fact, Gen Z is expected to overtake baby boomers in the workforce by next year, based on a 2024 survey by Glassdoor (Terrazas 2023).

With these generations forming the bulk of the global workforce, it's crucial for employers to understand their evolving expectations around work and purpose. According to the Deloitte 2024 Global Gen Z and Millennial Survey (Deloitte 2024), about 9 in 10 Gen Zs (86%) and millennials (89%) say having a sense of purpose in their work is very or somewhat important to their overall job satisfaction and well-being.

This sentiment directly impacts the war for talent: nearly as many (44% of Gen Zs and 40% of millennials) have declined job offers from employers who they perceive as having a negative environmental impact, contributing to inequality through non-inclusive practices, or lacking support for employees' mental well-being and work-life balance.

Moreover, three-quarters of Gen Zs and millennials (75%) consider an organization's community engagement and societal impact as important factors when evaluating potential employers.

The positive news is that many employers appear to be on the right track regarding purpose. Four in five Gen Zs (81%) and millennials (82%) report that their current job provides them with a sense of purpose. Additionally, 7 in 10 Gen Zs (71%) and millennials (72%) feel that their employers' values and purpose align with their own.

However, less than half of Gen Zs (49%) and millennials (47%) believe that businesses are having a positive impact on society. This highlights a gap between what these generations feel businesses are capable of and what they are currently delivering.

This gap indicates a significant opportunity for businesses to enhance their positive impact, thereby increasing engagement among the majority of their employees.

This belief is now being echoed by Paul Polman, the visionary former CEO of Unilever. He beautifully articulated the need for purpose as a crucial part of dealing with the existential crisis facing many companies. Polman told the *Washington Post* in 2015, "You see how many companies are searching for purpose, and how many have a short existence. The average length of a U.S. company is now 18 years. The average length of a CEO is less than four years. It's not

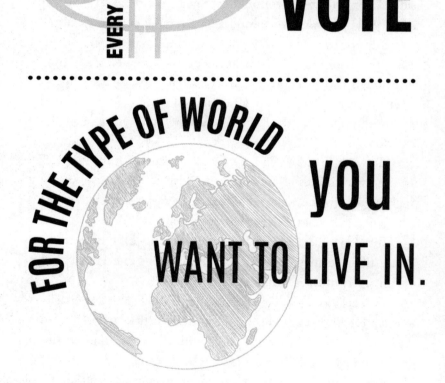

—Anne Lappe

just about making money, especially for the Millennial generation. They want to make a difference in life, so they look for companies that have a strong purpose" (Cunningham 2015).

Thus it is clear that building purpose-driven companies and brands that practice purpose-driven marketing is not only crucial for survival today but for ensuring you future-proof yourself for the next two generations of customers and talent.

The Disruptive Impact of Technology on Advertising

For years, the advertising model was based on finding out what consumers were paying attention to and creating ways to interrupt those experiences with a brand message. But people didn't want to be interrupted, especially with messages that weren't adding any value to their lives. So over the past two decades, smart innovators, frustrated with the intrusive nature of advertising, have given consumers the ability to control those interruptions, putting the power back in the hands of the people and creating a huge headache for traditional marketers.

At first DVRs allowed you to skip past ads on TV; now we have a new generation who are "cutting the cord" altogether and dispensing with conventional cable TV. According to a Pew Research Center survey, 19% of adults between the ages of 18 and 29 have become cord cutters, dropping cable or satellite TV service, while another 16% have never had a traditional subscription TV package (Horrigan and Duggan 2015). Today it is possible to buy an Apple TV and subscribe to new ad-free models such as Netflix, MAX, and Hulu—which means there is now a way never to have to see an ad on except for those who cannot afford the subscription fees and only have access to the ad tier version of these listed services.

Chapter 1: How Good Became the New Cool　35

But in 2024, the situation was even more dire, because of the massive rise of social media and its corresponding negative effects.

As of April 2024, there were 5.44 billion Internet users worldwide, which amounted to 67.1% of the global population. Of this total, 5.07 billion, or 62.6% of the world's population, were social media users (Petrosyan 2024).

As of 2024, the average daily social media usage of Internet users worldwide amounted to 143 minutes per day (Dixon 2024).

Concerns around social media are by now well established. Privacy issues arise from data breaches and unauthorized data sharing. Excessive use of social media can lead to anxiety, depression, and low self-esteem, particularly among adolescents. The rapid spread of misinformation and fake news on social platforms can influence public opinion and undermine trust in media. Additionally, social media can contribute to cyberbullying and online harassment, posing serious risks to users' safety and well-being.

All of these platforms are being underwritten by global advertising from corporations. Brands need to hold these media platforms (Facebook, Instagram, etc.) accountable for ensuring not just "brand safety" for their own brands—but ensuring that their media dollars are not supercharging the rise of societal dysfunction.

And by the way, consumers aren't loving brand advertising on social media either. According to HubSpot Research, 91% of people believe ads are more intrusive now compared to two or three years ago, and 79% believe they're being tracked by retargeted ads (An 2020).

With the unbelievably fast rise of artificial intelligence, marketers are again dealing with new challenges—from the ethics of whether to use the technology in the creation of advertising, which could lead to hundreds of thousands of jobs being lost in the creative industries, to ethical concerns around accountability, bias, and privacy. It makes it even more essential than ever before to ensure their brands are deeply rooted in purpose and values that ground them with integrity and humanity.

According to advertising giant Dentsu's Global Ad Spend Forecasts global advertising spend is now forecast to grow by 5.0% in 2024 (vs. 3.3% in 2023) to reach $754.4 billion in 2019 (Dentsu 2024). But with these generational and technological trends, conventional advertising and media is in danger of becoming irrelevant in the next few decades. Wouldn't it be amazing if we could find new models to channel that investment to marketing platforms that have a more positive and enduring effect? We believe we are at a crossroads: we can either choose to try to prop up an old model that is broken or we can create a new model that is fit for the unique challenges we see today.

The Crisis of Meaningfulness in Marketing

In addition to the massive generational and technological shifts, in the course of writing this book, we realized there is a fundamental spiritual shift happening within the marketing community.

Although businesses have made many meaningful contributions to the betterment of our world, it is also well documented that corporations have been responsible for all sorts of crimes against humanity, ranging from massive environmental damage and pollution to predatory mortgages to sweatshop labor.

Furthermore, while marketing has also been responsible for building brands and driving businesses that give millions of people jobs, many campaigns created by marketers have actually harmed humanity. Joe Camel and the Marlboro Man inspired generations of young people to start smoking, while Photoshopped imagery that created unrealistic and unattainable appearance goals caused body-image issues for generations of young girls. Marketers have helped to create a culture of materialistic excess that has led to the cancer of overconsumption. And even today marketers are all too often guilty of greenwashing or "brandwashing"—marketing their brands and corporations as paragons of virtue while ignoring insidious practices and reprehensible behavior behind the scenes.

We have reached a tipping point where the majority of the world hates what we do. In survey after survey, marketing is listed as one of the least valuable professions to humanity. An illuminating survey carried out by Adobe showed that 68% of people found advertising to be "annoying and distracting," with 53% reporting "most marketing is a bunch of bullshit" (Adobe 2012).

That same survey listed advertising/marketing as being among the bottom four most valuable professions to humanity (the top four being teacher, scientist, engineer, and social worker). What was most surprising was that the survey included people in the advertising/marketing profession—who were *more than twice as likely* as the average person to rank their profession as useless! It signals a deep *crisis of meaningfulness* in what we do for a living.

The desire to find more meaning in what we did for a living was the catalyst for us to start writing this book. And we realized we were not alone: in private conversations with our peers, many told us they were feeling professionally unfulfilled. As dreamers and doers who give brands voices, personalities, and power, they were rewarded well to use their talents to optimize profits, but they were increasingly inspired to optimize people's lives. We were all internally struggling with how to maintain a balance between being good marketers and being good citizens.

Chief Creative Officer at Tombras and winner of multiple awards, Jeff Benjamin is one of the most respected creatives in the advertising business. He had an epiphany one day he told us about: "I was watching the movie *Deep Impact*, about an asteroid hitting the Earth. In the movie, they create a shelter inside a mountain to safeguard the best of humanity—doctors, engineers, scientists. I was watching the movie, and it hit me . . . what I do for a living wouldn't help me make it into the mountain."

That's a great way to frame this problem: How do we do work that helps us make it into the mountain?

LEAST 4 VALUABLE PROFESSIONS TO SOCIETY

ADVERTISING/MARKETING
- 13%
- 35%

ACTOR/ACTRESS
- 13%
- 16%

DANCER
- 13%
- 15%

PR PROFESSIONAL
- 11%
- 23%

■ CONSUMERS
□ MARKETERS

Advertising/Marketing considered bottom four to consumers; not highly regarded by Marketing Professionals either

Chapter 2

The New Model of Marketing

The Time Is Now

Here's the good news: the idea that business has enormous potential to be a force for good is moving from niche to mainstream. Harvard Business School professor Michael Porter summarized the huge opportunity of the situation in a TED Talk titled "Why Business Can Be Good at Solving Social Problems." The following chart shows that by an order of magnitude, resources are concentrated in the hands of corporations.

This recognition of the power of corporations to drive positive social impact at scale is redefining the expectations of how corporations should behave.

In fact, we believe we are seeing a new evolution of capitalism—Conscious Capitalism—when customers, more than ever before, are demanding the brands and corporations in their lives demonstrate a positive effect on social issues. And to us the inference is simple: we believe Conscious Capitalism requires Conscious Marketing.

We believe the time is right for marketers to accept the challenge to lead organizations toward being forces for greater good. We believe marketers are exactly the kind of thoughtful, resourceful, versatile, inspirational people who are needed right now to address those inequities. We understand how to speak the languages of finance, R&D, sales, and marketing. We have the ability to speak to customers, understand what they need, spot market opportunities, and create propositions, products, and strategies for launching them into the world. We partner with designers, technologists, and artists to create conversations. We are well positioned to be the change makers in our organizations. Why, you may ask?

Marketers are the ones in an organization who are the champions of the customer. Practicing marketing like you actually give a damn about the lives of your customers means seeing what really matters to them. Nine times out of 10, it won't be another piece of

42 GOOD IS THE NEW COOL GUIDE TO MEANINGFUL MARKETING

WHERE ARE THE RESOURCES?

Total revenue by stakeholder, United States

NONPROFITS
$1.2 trillion

GOVERNMENT
$3.1 trillion

CORPORATIONS
$20.1 trillion

Source: Michael Porter TED.com

advertising; it will be something that helps them optimize their lives. In other words, we're saying not to use the tools of your trade to find ways to emotionally manipulate people; instead find ways to use the tools to inspire them, encourage them, and help them.

And in the process, we want to market like we give a damn about the wider impact marketing has on our neighborhoods and cities, on the environment and ecosystem. As the human population grows from 8 billion to an estimated 10 billion by 2050, and more and more people buy consumer products, the decisions we make as marketers—on product, on supply chain, on where marketing investments should flow—will have a profound impact. It is up to us to think in terms of marketing that delivers a triple bottom line in terms of profit, yes, but also in terms of people and planet.

To put it more bluntly: If we don't deal with income inequality, no one is going to be able to afford our products. If we don't deal with climate change, there's not going to be anybody left to buy them.

We think that in addition to the classical four *P*s of marketing (product, price, place, and promotion) there is now a fifth *P*: purpose. People want the brands they support to stand for more than profit, and they want to see that purpose brought to life in clear and tangible ways that benefit society and the planet. Today marketers have the responsibility to find ways to create purpose-driven marketing—and lead a team that not only includes their corporate social responsibility (CSR) counterparts but also CTOs, CFOs, and other leaders from every single part of the organization to radically rethink the ways in which their brands can do well by doing good. It is a golden opportunity to elevate marketing from being a profession that is hated to one that is admired.

But this new attitude needs a new model to make it work. The consumer expectation that brands do more good, coupled with the cool factor good now has, allows for smart marketers to develop big ideas that are cool, do good, and make money. This is creating disruption and opportunities not only in the way products are marketed but also in how they are developed, designed, and sold.

In our journey for this book, we met an inspiring new generation of marketers, social entrepreneurs, and culture creators who are out to change our world for the better. Sharing a collective sense of responsibility to help address the environmental, civic, and economic ills that are affecting all of us, these visionaries aspire not just to help change market conditions but also human conditions.

We were able to distill what they have learned into a model we think could replace the broken, traditional marketing model with something fresher and more meaningful.

How to Harness the Power of Cool

Building on our belief that "great marketing should optimize life," we think that today there is a powerful new model where brands ("commerce"), nonprofits ("conscience"), and artists ("culture") can work together to "make money and do good by harnessing the power of cool."

Each of these entities has valuable strengths. Brands with their budgets and customer bases have reach and resources; nonprofits have in-depth knowledge of how to solve issues and armies of workers and volunteers dedicated to their cause; and artists have the ability to shine a spotlight on an issue, and help engage their fan bases.

Working together allows us to solve issues within each of our own industries. Brands that genuinely find purpose and align themselves with nonprofits and artists to create large-scale, meaningful ways to solve people's problems will be able to solve the "trust gap" with consumers and turn them into their biggest advocates. Artists who partner with brands and nonprofits in sustainable and respectful ways can use their talents to not only give them new canvases but also leave behind a moral legacy as well as an artistic one. And social entrepreneurs who create alliances of integrity with the right artists and brands can find ways to use the power of cool to do more good than if they tried on their own.

We all need each other to make what we do more meaningful, more powerful, and reach more people. To do that, we should follow these seven principles.

1. Know Your Purpose: The greatest companies today have a higher-order purpose than just profit. Tesla's is "To accelerate the world's transition to sustainable energy," and Nike's is "To bring inspiration and innovation to every athlete in the world." Think about how inspiring these purposes are to the customers and employees of these companies—far more than any quarterly profit goal. Finding your brand's higher-order purpose is the first step to unlocking a tremendous amount of meaning and potential.

2. Find Your Allies: Today's brands must build coalitions of allies with common purpose—especially with nonprofits (who bring an in-depth knowledge of how to solve issues) and "architects of cool" (who are able to shine a cultural spotlight and ignite societal change). That's a terrifically powerful way to tackle the massive problems facing the world today. As the African proverb says, "If you want to go fast, go alone. If you want to go far, go together."

3. Think Citizens, Not Consumers: We believe that if you only treat people as consumers of your product, you are condemned to have only a one-dimensional relationship with them. Conversely,

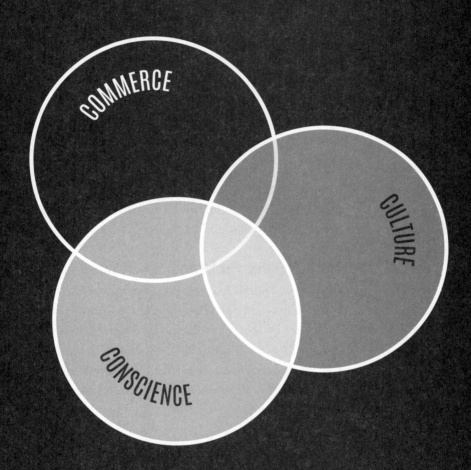

if you treat people as citizens—with a range of passions, concerns, and goals—you will be able to have a much richer, multidimensional relationship with them. In that relationship your purpose as a brand can find common ground with their purpose; instead of being in a transactional relationship, you can be in a transformational relationship.

4. Lead with the Cool: Today it is no longer just enough for a brand to be good; it must also be cool. It must have great design and a great story, and it must be an object of desire. People don't buy Warby Parker glasses just because buying a pair donates another pair to a person in need. They buy them because they have amazing designs at great prices, conveniently available online or in great store experiences. Smart, socially impactful brands from Method to Tesla know the "power of cool" in helping shift behavior.

5. Don't Advertise, Solve Problems: Instead of just defaulting to advertising as the solution to everything, we believe the natural intersection that brands can and should focus on is adding value to their consumers' lives by solving problems. These problems could range from the everyday (e.g. time-saving services and products) to the epic (e.g. ending poverty, income inequality, or environmental pollution). What brands choose to work on depends on their organizational purpose and goals.

6. People Are the New Media: In an age of increasing ad blocking, how do you communicate your message at scale? According to a study by Nielsen, 92% of people trust recommendations from friends and family more than all other forms of marketing (Nielsen 2012). And 81% of US online customers' purchase decisions are influenced by their friends' social media posts (Scanlan 2012). Marketers should be obsessive about creating marketing experiences,

THE "GOOD IS THE NEW COOL" MODEL
GREAT MARKETING OPTIMIZES LIFE

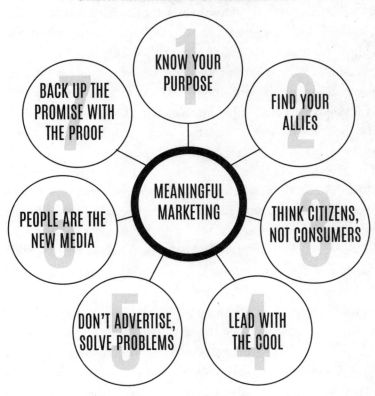

HOW TO MAKE MONEY AND DO GOOD
BY HARNESSING THE
POWER OF COOL

products, and services that are so good people will want to spontaneously tell their friends, coworkers, and family about them.

7. Back Up the Promise with the Proof: "Young people have been marketed to since they were babies, they develop this incredibly sophisticated bullshit detector, and the only way to circumvent the bullshit detector is to not bullshit," says Vice founder Shane Smith (2014). Make sure you back up the promise of the brand (your marketing communication) with the proof (actual tangible evidence of the good you are doing). Otherwise, your customers and community will expose it for the empty rhetoric it is.

TO SUMMARIZE OUR POINT OF VIEW: Instead of creating yet more advertising, your goal should be to create purpose-based marketing experiences and services that are so inspirational, educational, or useful that they create an army of advocates to help spread the story of your brand in a rich, authentic way. That's how we think "great marketing optimizes life," and that's how marketers can find more meaningfulness in the work they do.

In the next couple of chapters, we're going to cover the greatest allies brands have: the architects of cool and the new nonprofits. When they all work together, they create an amazing opportunity to "make money and do Good by harnessing the power of cool."

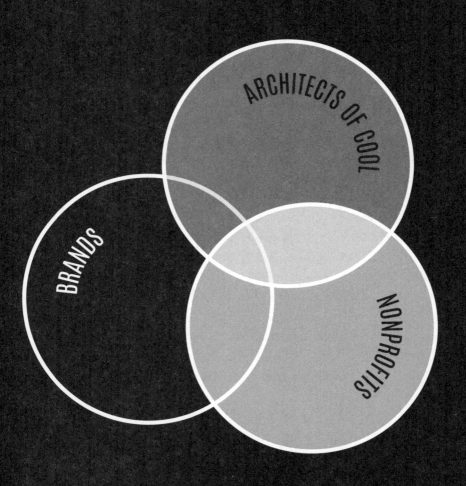

The Architects of Cool Are on Your Side

Here's some more good news for brands: the architects of cool are on your side.

Who are the architects of cool? We classify them as cultural entrepreneurs, storytellers, and artists (whether in the fields of music, film, visual art, or others), designers (in the fields of fashion, products, and architecture), and others (athletes, journalists). They are the people who drive culture forward, who help shape the popular agenda, who define the indefinable *cool*. Beyond being simply the engine of entertainment, there is a growing realization that cool should also be a force for good. We see these architects of cool increasingly using their fame, reach, and resources to drive global awareness and change across areas such as public health, youth advocacy, and education. As Lady Gaga says, "I don't want to make money; I want to make a difference" (Blasberg 2011). And the architects of cool can become some of your greatest allies in this new model.

Many of today's leading culture creators have realized they can and should contribute something that is more tangible than another record or movie—from Harry Styles partnership with Everytown for Gun Safety to Selena Gomez's Rare Beauty brand which raises money for mental health.

Using cool to do good has a long history, whether you look at the Concert for Bangladesh organized by Ravi Shankar and Beatle George Harrison or the legendary Live Aid concerts of the 1980s. But beyond these models, the architects of cool have found all-new ways to leverage their fame for positive social impact. Later in the book we'll look at Bono's (PRODUCT)RED, an artist-created social-good platform that allowed myriad brands, such as Apple, Nike, Starbucks, and the Gap, to get involved in the fight against HIV/AIDS.

I DON'T WANT TO MAKE

MONEY

I WANT TO MAKE A

Difference

— Lady Gaga

In fact, for the architects of cool looking to create social impact at scale, brands with their financial resources and huge reach have become their partners of choice. Later in the book, we'll explore how Lady Gaga's Born This Way Foundation has partnered with brands ranging from Mattel to Viacom.

The architects of cool include designers who are making beautiful, desirable products that also have a net social good. Designers such as Apple's Jonathan Ive and Yves Béhar have helped put design at the forefront of popular culture. Béhar in particular has been a vocal proponent of this idea, stating, "Design needs a new relationship with the world, one that is more focused on our planet's needs" (Perlroth 2011).

From packaging and interfaces to architecture and wearable technology, designers are applying the lessons from William McDonough's Cradle to Cradle movement, which posits that good design isn't just about surface aesthetics; it's also about having a deep understanding of how and where your products are made and what their long-term impact on the planet will be. Later in the book, we'll talk to Marco Vega from the small agency We Believers, which has been making big waves recently with its creation of edible six-pack rings for beer companies (the rings become food for aquatic life), helping reduce the amount of harmful plastic waste in the ocean.

Whether it's Lady Gaga or a sneaker designer sitting down to her first day of work at Nike, these architects of cool now increasingly have a new mission—how to use their power of cool to do good.

TOMORROW IS ALWAYS ANOTHER

DAY

TO MAKE THINGS RIGHT

LAURYN HILL

DESIGN needs a new relationship with the world, one that is more focused on our planet's **NEEDS.**

—Yves Béhar

The New Nonprofits

In addition to the architects of cool, there is another extremely important set of players that brands should consider partnering with—the nonprofits of the world. Historically, brands have either seen nonprofits only as recipients of corporate largesse—receiving donations from corporate social responsibility programs—or as a partner to carry out some sort of "cause-marketing" initiative. This is not to denigrate those CSR or cause-marketing programs but is instead to encourage brands to go beyond these traditional models and see nonprofits as partners that can bring a unique set of complementary skills to the task of "making money and doing good."

What excites us is a new wave of nonprofits being run by a new generation of leaders who are open to building coalitions and alliances between brands and artists that have never been seen before. Perhaps the biggest difference is their unwillingness to see the world in traditional terms. Take, for instance, Adam Braun, the CEO of Pencils of Promise, one of the most audacious and entrepreneurial start-ups to emerge in recent years. Adam's journey began with a child begging in the streets of India asking him for a pencil. This simple exchange inspired him to create a nonprofit that has achieved an amazing amount of success in a short time.

Adam's enlightened worldview is also bolstered by the techniques he brought with him after years of working in the finance and management-consultancy industries. Adam and his team run Pencils of Promise with a level of accountability and efficiency that would shame many for-profit businesses. The success of this approach can be seen in the fact that at the time this book is going to press, not only can Pencils of Promise claim to have built 342 schools—serving 33,883 students since 2009—they are also breaking ground on new schools at the frankly astonishing rate of one every 90 hours.

This results-driven, transparent approach has also brought on corporate partners ranging from fashion brands such as Warby Parker,

Dolce & Gabbana, and Versace to media brands such as AOL, Vogue, and Google. And thanks to Adam's brother Scooter Braun (whom we interview later in the book), who manages a certain Mr. Justin Bieber, Pencils of Promise has also gained a huge amount of publicity and traction among a younger audience, through Justin's support and advocacy of the program.

Another great example of a nonprofit that takes a fresh and radical approach is "charity: water," started by former nightclub entrepreneur Scott Harrison. After a decade of debauchery in the New York club scene, Scott had an epiphany one New Year's Day that led him to start volunteering as a photojournalist on the Mercy Ships, a floating hospital serving the people of Liberia. What he saw on that trip profoundly changed him. He came back and was inspired to throw a birthday party celebration where his guests were invited to donate money to clean water wells in Africa. The response was so great it led him to found charity: water, which to date has raised more than $740 million from passionate supporters and donors, enough to bring clean water to more than 16.8 million people. These projects have saved millions of people from having to walk miles to get water from unsafe sources, saving them time and improving their health in exponential ways.

Scott runs the organization more like a start-up than a traditional nonprofit. Log on to charity: water's website and you see design and branding that would be the envy of many brands. The design is clean and consistent, and well-thought-out assets—from press kits to campaign materials to videos—are easily downloadable and shareable. This sophisticated brand-led approach has also brought on board sponsors such as American Express, Caterpillar, and Nautica.

A great example of a nonprofit that has mastered how to harness the power of cool is Global Citizen, which was started by Hugh Evans, a young man from Australia, with the inspiring goal of ending the extreme poverty of 1.2 billion people (around 20% of the world's population). At the age of 14, he returned from a visit to a slum in Manila and announced to his mother that he wanted to dedicate his life to ending extreme poverty.

Hugh's strategy has involved staging large-scale music festivals on the Great Lawn of Central Park: the 2016 edition included music from Rihanna, Kendrick Lamar, Metallica, and Major Lazer and corporate partners such as Gucci Chime for Change, Johnson and Johnson, and Live Nation. You may think this sounds like a pretty traditional approach, similar to Live 8, in that it acted as a catalyst for world leaders meeting at the UN to commit to financial and legislative packages to help end extreme poverty. But the added twist was that you couldn't buy a ticket to the concert—you could only earn one by performing a range of actions, from watching and sharing videos about a topic to donating money to charities such as UNICEF and Rotary International.

In 2024, we're delighted to see a huge array of amazing nonprofits in the world doing innovative work—in fact, we profile a couple of them (Choose Love and Rivet) in this book. Nonprofits have in-depth knowledge of a particular problem and how to solve it; they have experts and resources in the places that need them the most. Nonprofits have communities that have a deep sense of purpose and belief in their missions, which are willing to go to extreme lengths and make great sacrifices to help others. As brands become more useful and start to tackle some of the biggest problems of humanity—climate change, poverty, equality for all—they would be foolish to discount nonprofits as key partners that can complement their scale, reach, and resources.

Chapter 2: The New Model of Marketing   59

Part II

The Seven Principles of How to Market Like You Give a Damn

Chapter 3

Know Your Purpose

We start with what is probably the most important principle: Know Your Purpose. Whether it's your personal purpose in life or your organization's purpose, it's important to be clear about what it is—and how it can be of service to others. True Purpose is always in service to something bigger than yourself.

Love him or hate him, Elon Musk—the founder of hugely purpose-driven companies Tesla, SpaceX, and SolarCity, among others—puts it another way: "Putting in long hours for a corporation is hard. Putting in long hours for a cause is easy."

In this section, we discover how entrepreneur Scooter Braun finds common purpose in all the work he does—whether for his artists, the people who work for him, or the philanthropic work he does. Peter McGuiness shares how Chobani built a billion-dollar brand based on the values of inclusivity, respect, and genuine concern for others' well-being. And Amy Smith, chief brand officer at the revered TOMS, shares how the company evolved its Purpose to keep up with the changing times.

Scooter Braun

Founder, SB Projects

How did Purpose go from the subject of academic journals and TED Talks to something that is now part of pop culture? Well, some of the credit must lie with Scooter Braun, who first discovered Justin Bieber as a 12-year-old singing on YouTube. After signing him to his management company, he steered Justin from his early days through his infamous rocky adolescence back to his current-day dominance of the charts. Braun and Bieber have partnered on one of the greatest redemption stories in pop music, though at the heart of this wasn't some calculated strategy but a genuine journey of finding true Purpose. Using the power of music, Scooter has been able to open up the idea of Purpose to a whole new generation of young people.

It's a packed concert amphitheater in Seattle, and the biggest pop star in the world, Justin Bieber, is standing onstage in front of a white grand piano and a crowd of 16,000 fans. It's the opening night of his world tour, and he is speaking from the heart about how he lost his Purpose and found it again, before launching into the song "Purpose," from his hit album of the same name. The crowd goes wild, singing along to every line.

Named one of *Time* magazine's 100 Most Influential People, Scooter Braun has diversified his portfolio via his company, SB Projects, which not only manages talent like Kanye West, Black Eyed Peas, Tori Kelly, Martin Garrix, and Karlie Kloss but also invests in new film and television projects and technology start-ups. Even though he manages some of the most famous people on the planet, Scooter is remarkably down-to-earth and willing to share his life experience. We talk about his own journey in life and what kind of expectations he had, starting from his early high school years.

"I was on the basketball team, I was class president, I was a social kid. People had all these expectations of what I was going to become. They would tell me all the time. When I went to college, it was that pressure of everyone wanting me to become great . . . I worked out of fear. I operated on the idea that what if I didn't live up to their expectations? 'I can't fail. Failure is not an option.' I would work endlessly because I was so scared of failure and not because I was excited for success. That's what drove me. Every time I reached one new achievement, I was on to the next one quickly, because it was never enough. I had a couple of pivotal moments in my life. One was when a buddy of mine died. He was actually killed just after we left a nightclub, and I said to myself, 'I've got to change my life.'"

After that sobering experience, Scooter's drive in life evolved from being one of a fear of failure to a more financial one—hitting the "number."

Scooter says, "I was 19 when I started my business. When I was 23 I met a guy who had a house, a beautiful family, a dog, and a little whaler boat; I thought he had the perfect life. I said, 'How much money do you need to live this lifestyle?' And he sat me down and told me the amount of money required to live that lifestyle. It's not as much as you think. It takes millions of dollars, but it's not that insane. The number he gave me became my lifetime goal: 'I'm set if I get to that point, and if I double it then I'm beyond set.' I thought I'd work until my fifties to get there."

Scooter recalls the unforgettable moment in his life when he realized he had reached his goal. "When I was twenty-seven years old I was driving down the street in Atlanta when my accountant called. I asked him, 'How much money do I have across all my accounts?' and he named a number higher than my lifetime goal. I was twenty-seven. I said, 'Thank you' and hung up the phone. I felt no joy and I started becoming incredibly depressed, because I realized nothing had changed, my life was continuing to go on, nothing had moved."

At that moment of truth, he called on one of the people who had influenced him most in life. "I pulled over to the side of the road and called my dad, and I said, 'I want to tell you my lifetime goal. I've achieved that already. I'm really depressed because nothing changed. I always thought if I got there, I wouldn't feel the pressure, I'd feel joy. But I feel nothing.' My father said one of the wisest things he's ever said to me. He said, 'I want you to do me a favor. I want you to hang up the phone and I want you to think back over the last few years about when you were really happy, and I want you to call me back.' I said, 'What?' and he said, 'Just do it.'"

Scooter continues, "I hung up the phone. I thought about it, called him back two minutes later, and said, 'It's going to sound cheesy, but what really makes me happy are the seemingly small moments that create special experiences for others like playing basketball with old friends, giving away concert tickets, and randomly answering feedback from fans on Facebook.' He said, 'Implement more of that into your life. You can't change what you do or who you are, but you can implement more of the things that actually give you joy into your life.' That was a very big turning point for me. I understood that I don't do this to make money. The joy comes from these things that I implement into that work from the giveback projects that we do to the Saturday morning basketball ritual I have. The joy I have of seeing not only my artists succeed but also the team at SB Projects getting their first platinum plaques and having their own victories. It became about recognizing that joy and implementing more of it into my life."

Another profound realization came with the birth of his son, Jagger. "By making life for the first time I understood what death was. My purpose became very real for the first time: put as much of the good things in me into that person as I can until I die. To give as much back to the world as I can before I die, because someday I will no longer exist." He pauses to reflect on the title of this book, *Good Is the New Cool*, and how it relates to the vision of his life. He says, "So we've been talking about what 'cool' is and what is 'good.' Different people can interpret both of those words in many different ways. Is being good doing something you should just do anyway, like being a good father? It's like the famous Chris Rock line, 'Do you want a cookie? For being a good dad?' People are going to interpret 'good' in a different way. I'm hoping to reinforce the idea that you can be successful in this industry and be a good, loving family man."

He continues, "My job isn't to be remembered. My job is to leave a positive impact through my family and my work, because I don't think we get remembered. I think some people get remembered more than others, but eventually we all get forgotten. Your legacy isn't about you; it's about the impact you can leave. I vividly remember sitting there and having this amazing awakening of

68 GOOD IS THE NEW COOL GUIDE TO MEANINGFUL MARKETING

'Oh my God, I will not be here someday.' So what is it for? It's to do something worthwhile while I'm here. It's when people say, 'I don't remember Scooter Braun' but they're doing something with their lives in a positive manner, without them even knowing maybe I played a role in that. If I can die knowing that I made that effort, then that's my purpose."

Scooter extends this philosophy to motivating the people who work for him at SB Projects. He says, "It's funny, I feel like I work for them now. I don't need to work anymore. If I chose, I could just stay at home with my family for the rest of my life. There's no amount of money that's going to change my lifestyle. I go to work now to not only see how great we can be but also because there are people who work for me because their paycheck means they can put food in their kid's mouth or a roof over their own head. Just because I've 'won' doesn't mean we've all 'won' yet. So now, the same people who helped me get to where I want to go, now it's my job—I've got to reach down my hand and say, 'OK, let's go. I'm not going anywhere, I'm not going to run off. Now I'm going to reach down and I'll pull you up.'"

This approach may be part of the reason Scooter and his SB Projects team have been so successful in negotiating brand partnerships for his artists. Justin alone has had brand deals with Adidas, Beats by Dre, Best Buy, T-Mobile, Schmidt's, and Vespa. The values that serve as a foundation for SB Projects are on the company's website for everyone to see. They include such aphorisms as "Family is everything," "Superhuman work ethic #hustle and #grind," and "Find your meaning and make it count." Scooter applies these principles to all his artists, helping them translate their emotions into an art form that is loved by people around the world.

He says, "I think that's my job with all of them. I'm not doing it for money. The job is to help them. They're giving one of the most raw art forms a person possibly can to the world, which is their

My job isn't to be
REMEMBERED.

My job is to leave a
POSITIVE IMPACT
through my family
and my work.

—SCOOTER BRAUN

music—they're baring their souls in a way that translates beyond language. That's why when we go to countries where people don't speak English, they're singing every lyric to the songs. They're basically pouring out emotions. My job is to help them convey that—and to do so in a way [that makes them] feel comfortable."

Scooter has also always had a strong philanthropic streak in him, something that runs in the family. As mentioned, his brother Adam is the founder of the progressive and successful nonprofit Pencils of Promise, and Justin Bieber has been a loyal supporter, donating his time and energy to raising money for the organization. Bieber has also earmarked funds from some of his licensing deals—his Someday perfume, for example—for Pencils of Promise, as well as donating a dollar from every ticket sold on one of his concert tours to the philanthropic nonprofit. Another little known fact is that Justin is one of Make-A-Wish Foundations top wish-granters, with over 250 appearances to his name.

Scooter moves on to talk about how he and Justin came up with the theme of "Purpose" and how it came to life with the album. "We each came to understand how the theme of purpose was integral to the album in our own ways. As I helped write the song 'Purpose,' I kept coming back to the major themes in one of my favorite books, Viktor Frankl's *Man's Search for Meaning*. He was a Holocaust survivor and psychiatrist who survived through the war, survived Auschwitz, and wrote this book. It talks about the idea that the most powerful thing we have is purpose. And the ones who survived the camps weren't the ones with the most money or the most strength . . . [they were] the ones who had something to live for. When their purpose got taken away, if they were living for their wife and they found out their wife died, they'd quickly die after because they'd lost their purpose."

Man's Search for Meaning has an added layer of meaning for Scooter because his grandparents were also Holocaust survivors. He says, "I started looking at how powerful it was to me and I started thinking about how the best-selling books in the world—like the Bible, for instance—are all based on purpose. I said we should make a song about that because Justin was trying to figure out what this is all for—his purpose. So I started giving Poo Bear, the song's producer and cowriter, all these lines that he built on before showing Justin."

He continues, "Justin loved it. He changed a few words and wrote some personal stuff for him, and that's how the song idea came about. Once he recorded it, he called me up and asked, 'I'm thinking about naming the album *Purpose*. What do you think?' I said, 'It's really amazing for me to hear you say that because that song was very important to me because of [Frankl's] book, but what does it mean to you, because it's your album?' He said, 'I like that it had multiple meanings; I like the fact that it's personal to you. You know, I want it to be personal to my fans.'"

And indeed it has been. Scooter says, "I've been there for his first three . . . shows in this past week, and every single night he plays 'Purpose' last before the encore. And every night he talks and he says, 'Please, if there is anything you take away from this, it's that you should look for the most important thing: purpose,' and he goes, 'I lost mine. I have it now; thanks to all you guys, I found it again. Whatever your purpose is, strive for it.'"

When asked about whether there is a common thread among all the work Scooter does—whether it is managing his talent, his business ventures, or his philanthropic work—Scooter pauses and turns reflective. He says, "There's something my great-grandmother used to say to me, which is, 'Maturity is knowing that your twelve-year-old self is just fine.' You know, this idea of who you always were, it's OK to be that person. I've always been the person—I think Justin has too, we kind of share this—if we go to a comedy, a movie theater . . . we'll laugh, but we'll also turn to see if everyone else is laughing. Everyone laughing won't make us laugh, but we don't get as much joy unless they are. So the common thing between all this is, what's the point of laughing alone? It's this idea of 'sharing joy.'"

Why We Love This Example: "Sharing joy." It's as simple as that. Scooter's journey through being driven by the expectations of others, fear of failure, and the desire to hit financial success is an all-too-common one. Sometimes it takes tragedy, such as the death of someone close to you, and sometimes it takes profound joy, such as the birth of a child, but the clarity always comes at a certain point. True Purpose is always in service to somebody or something else; Purpose is never for yourself. Scooter's Purpose is in service to his family, his artists, and his employees; Justin Bieber's is to his fans and to his craft. By acknowledging their gifts and passions are there to help people other than themselves, they find true meaning and satisfaction.

Peter McGuinness,
President, Chobani

Chobani is one of America's most admired brands. In many ways, the company embodies the American dream—founded by an immigrant entrepreneur who built a company from the ground up to be the biggest yogurt brand in the country. But this barely scratches the surface of what makes this company great. Its president and chief operating officer, Peter McGuiness shares how Chobani built a billion-dollar brand based on the values of inclusivity, respect, and genuine concern for others' well-being.

The Chobani story begins on a cold January day in 2005 on a quiet road in Upstate New York. Its founder, a Turkish immigrant named Hamdi Ulukaya, is driving down a nondescript street, past a street sign that reads Dead End, where he finds his destination, an old factory building that had recently been closed after 85 years. The structure is for sale, and the business is closing. The owners of the yogurt plant no longer saw any value in the building and were practically giving it away to anyone who would take it off their hands. But what struck Hamdi as he looked around the space was not the sight of an abandoned building; it was the sight of abandoned people. Fifty-five employees of the factory were losing their jobs. They had spent decades of their lives building this business, and their only remaining task was to ensure the plant was closed forever. Like the street's signpost warned, this was supposed to be the end of their road, which infuriated Hamdi.

He saw something in these people. He saw integrity, pride, worth, and a willingness to work to build a better life for themselves and others. He believed in them, and a few days later, he decided to borrow money to buy the building and start a yogurt business. He used the money to hire five of those employees, eventually hiring all of them. Their first order of business was to go to Ace Hardware and buy paint. Hamdi joked in his 2019 TED Talk that it was the only idea he had of what to do. Together, they painted the outside walls white, a clean slate for a new business that would always recognize and honor the value of people, especially those who have been given up on by others.

Since that day, Chobani has become the maker of America's number-one-selling Greek yogurt brand in the United States. *People* magazine recognized Chobani as one of the top "50 Companies That Care in 2018," and *Fortune* has recognized Chobani as one of the top 50 companies changing the world. It now employs thousands of employees, and for three consecutive years, Chobani has been a certified Great Place to Work.

Chobani follows one of the key principles we espouse—"Know Your Purpose." The company starts with its employees: paying double the minimum wage in its factories and creating a shared-equity platform, which means employees own 10% of the $2 billion company. The goal, the founder has said, is to pass along the wealth they have helped build in the decade since the company started. According to reports, at its $3 billion valuation, the average employee payout would be $150,000. The earliest employees, though, will most likely be given many more shares, possibly worth over $1 million.

Befitting a company started by an immigrant, Chobani is also hugely supportive of immigrants and refugees. It set up the Tent Foundation, which tries to mobilize the private sector to improve the livelihoods of the more than 25 million men and women forcibly displaced from their home countries, as well as numerous other initiatives around inclusivity, veterans, social justice, and sustainability. In doing so, it has become an iconic brand that rivals Ben & Jerry's in its authentic approach to doing good in the world.

We wanted to learn how Chobani has grown from its humble beginnings to one of the most successful and respected American brands, so we spoke with Peter McGuinness, its president. Passionate, provocative, and innovative, Peter is one of the leading voices championing the idea that business can be a force for good. (2024 Update: He's since gone on to become president and CEO of another mission-driven brand, Impossible Foods.)

Peter began by talking about the Purpose of Chobani. "'Better Food for More People' is the founding mission and vision of the company. And this was based on an insight that people have good taste; they just need good options. Good food is a right, not a privilege. We thought that 'delicious, nutritious, natural, affordable' was the future of food. But there's an inherent paradox embedded in that purpose statement that creates space for innovation and growth."

He explains what he means. "It's a little bit more of a loaded equation than you may think. It's hard from a profitability and supply chain perspective. That's a very tricky finance equation because our cost of goods is higher, our sourcing is better, and we're straining our yogurt (three cups of milk to one cup of yogurt). So we're not adding gelatin and thickeners; we're not adding artificial preservatives or cheap artificial sweeteners. We're using high-quality ingredients, but we don't want to price it out of the reach of everybody. So, I think it's a really noble mission to want to do 'better food for more people,' which is basically nutritional wellness. A 'wellness company' is how we view ourselves, and we want 'universal wellness' to happen sooner."

This rearticulation has led to the adoption of "universal wellness" as Chobani's North Star. "What we mean by making 'universal wellness' happen sooner is first, nutritional wellness—secondly, social wellness: immigration, equality, inclusion, our employees, our communities. And thirdly, environmental wellness. And so how we've distilled down our company is that we are a food-focused wellness company that uses food as a force of good."

Deep at the core of Chobani lies a set of core values that drive everything the company does. "If it's just on a screen or on a piece of paper, that means absolutely nothing to me. You need to live it day in and day out. Deeds are louder than words, you know? At Chobani, it's very, very genuine; it's very, very natural. It doesn't look like we're being exploitative or commercial, because we've kind of always been about that. So it's not questioned; it doesn't look like a stunt. We're not trying to do this stuff to seem cool when we're not. We're not trying to do this stuff to seem like we have a heart, and we don't. This is how we live. This is how we work. This courses through our veins at Chobani," he shared.

This core belief naturally manifests so strongly in everything the company does that it doesn't even have a CSR department. Peter laughs. "We don't have a corporate responsibility department. I don't even know what the hell that is. That's our entire company, not a department. On all the good stuff we've done, we've never done anything paid behind it. A third of our workforce are refugees and immigrants. We don't do ads about that. If it's truly who you are at the core, you don't need to brag about it. If people find out organically, great, but we weren't doing it for that reason. I think that's the real difference."

Peter is thoughtful when he talks about how a brand can embody kindness and tolerance while also being a fierce competitor commercially. "I think you can be a warrior and a shepherd. 'Chobani' means 'shepherd' (in Turkish). And I think shepherds give the shirt off their back, and it's very unconditional. And then I think you can also be a fierce warrior and want to win in the marketplace. I think that the same company can want to do good in the world and help humanity. I don't think that those are two divergent thoughts anymore."

Peter is also quick to admit that the brand made some missteps along the way. "We've made some mistakes in the past where we're super righteous and called out our competition. We had the right to do it and had the science behind us, and you know what? Consumers didn't really like it if you're righteous and from the mountaintop. It's yogurt. So, I don't think you can take yourself too seriously." This lesson led to the realization that Chobani didn't have to wear its values on its sleeve.

"I think you can have packaging that's accessible and approachable and fun because so much of that's in the brand and almost goes without saying from a consumer perspective. You don't have to express all that in the packaging. We don't have to be uber-serious and have a million different claims about nutrition. And if you look at our core cup, it's just beautiful fruit. We don't talk about things like 'two billion probiotics' like it's a science experiment. We want our food to be good to eat, fun to eat," he said.

Peter pauses as he thinks about what advice he'd give to other purpose-driven leaders in the space. "I think everybody should have their own playbook and what works for Chobani may not work for many, many other companies. Find that one thing that is beautiful about your brand or your business, and double down on it. Every brand has something that's magical about it. Stop trying to search for the next thing. Stop trying to reinvent stuff, unearth something very magical that's there and authentic and real. And that could be a founder story, it could be a founding belief, a founding principle, it could be a cultural trait. Don't do it because it's on trend or because you think it could be exploited. Do it because it's something special and sincere and genuine about that brand. Champion it. Make everybody live it so that it becomes this prideful, galvanizing thing that later can manifest itself in the external world."

Finally, we asked Peter to summarize Chobani in one word.

"Humanity. That's what we stand for. We're advocates of humanity in terms of how we treat our plant workers or employees. How we make our products, how we treat the planet in terms of the community, the disaster relief work we do, our hiring practices, our foundation work, our refugee and immigrant stances, our sexual and gender orientations stances. Just speak your values and views and have a point of view. If your culture is that, let it fly. Do the right thing, regardless of short-term impacts. By doing that, have we upset some people along the way that may have consumed yogurt? Yes. But that's what we believe. And we think it's the right thing to do."

Why We Love This Example: In many ways, the story of Chobani's beginning tells you all you need to know about the Purpose and values that guide the brand and the company to this day. It's no surprise that a business started by an immigrant—and displaced employees forced to leave the company they called home—would build a business that employs refugees and champions causes such as immigration, equality, and inclusion. At the core of everything, Chobani does believe that people deserve better. They treated their first employees with dignity and care, and in turn, their employees built a multibillion-dollar business by providing better food for more people. They have proved that you can serve society like a shepherd and compete in the industry as a warrior, especially when that is who you most authentically are at your core.

Amy Smith

Chief Brand Officer, TOMS

Fashion brand TOMS is steadfast in its pursuit of progress over perfection. We sat down with Amy Smith, chief giving officer at TOMS, to discuss the evolution of the company Purpose, the risks they have taken to stand up for what they believe is right, and what they have learned along their journey.

TOMS have been one of the trailblazers in the business-for-good space for over two decades, pioneering the one-for-one model of giving, which has proved so successful that the company has now donated 93 million pairs of shoes since inception, not to mention giving millions of dollars to causes as well (the company donates between 40% and 50% of net profits, the highest percentage of any US company).

Their chief brand officer, Amy Smith, is one of our favorite people. She is upbeat and optimistic, with a heart of gold. She's hosted hundreds of changemakers at our first GOOD IS THE NEW COOL conference at the TOMS office and has always been generous with her time and wisdom, while at the same time being open to what TOMS is seeking to learn. Amy talked about how TOMS sees its role as proving that business and social impact can happen at scale.

"I feel incredibly grateful that my journey has brought me here. I'm so excited to see if a company like TOMS that gives at an unprecedented level can scale, can continue to give at that kind of a level. Because I think, then we can hopefully be kind of the inspiration (or at least guinea pig) for other companies that are trying to do this. And there's lots of small, amazing companies out there doing this. But I don't know if any of us have cracked the nut of going to scale," she began.

At inception, the company expanded (some would say too quickly) beyond shoes into eyewear, coffee, water, backpacks, and watchbands (each tackling a different issue, like vision for eyewear, bullying for backpacks, and solar light for watchbands) in an attempt to create a truly socially conscious lifestyle brand for millennials. This led to a moment of internal self-reflection. "We really got to this point of, hold on: maybe having a new give and a new product every year, it might not make sense for us. And so we've since then been taking a pause to say, are we having as much impact as we possibly can have with this level of giving?"

After pioneering the one-for-one model (which was so successful that at one point, there were an estimated 1,800 companies who had adopted it as their giving model), TOMS reached an inflection point that led to the company for the first time exploring new models and issues. Amy recalled, "When I joined, the first question I asked was 'Are there any sacred cows?' Like I assumed, if I brought that question to Blake [Mycoskie, the founder], he would say, 'Don't touch one-for-one.' Right? And he didn't. He didn't because he's an incredibly self-aware, passionate, driven-by-the-impact person. And so that really opened the door for us to explore where else might we have an impact."

That first bold step came in the form of tackling gun violence—sparked by founder Blake Mycoskie's reaction to the Thousand Oaks shooting. Amy spoke passionately about the call to action and partnering with amazing organizations such as the Black and Brown Gun Violence Prevention Consortium, Everytown for Gun Safety, Faith in Action, Giffords: Courage to Fight Gun Violence, March for Our Lives, Moms Demand Action, and Live Free. "If you know anything about the ending gun violence space, pretty much anyone and everyone you've talked to calls it 'the moment.' It's the moment where you say, 'That's enough. That's the end. I have to do something.' And for Blake and his family, that moment was the Thousand Oaks shooting."

The speed of the decision meant that the company had to learn fast. "It was a wild ride because it was quick. So the first ten days we talked to over forty partners. I literally would answer the phone to anyone that would call me back." We asked Amy about what she learned from the process of onboarding a cause so quickly within a corporate environment.

So the first is, surround yourself with the experts, and do it really, really fast. We're not the experts, we will never be the experts in this, but we've got to learn as fast as we can. The second is to be humble. The third is to put your money where your mouth is. We invested $5 million in supporting ending gun violence, which is the largest corporate gift given to date. And then the last point was to provide a place for your supporters to engage. And so along with the financial investment, we also invited our supporters to come to TOMS.com and to complete a postcard that we ultimately hand-delivered to the House of Representatives, urging them to pass HR8, which is the universal background check bill."

Over 730,000 people completed a postcard, which showed the appetite for action among the TOMS community, especially among younger millennials and Gen Z.

Amy is clear eyed about the pros and cons of taking on such a politically sensitive topic: "Ending gun violence, although it could be perceived as a real political issue, for us, it's a human issue. One hundred people in America die every single day because of gun violence. One hundred people. As we sit here chatting, we will have lost two or three people in the United States to gun violence. That's not okay. There's nothing about that that is okay. And there's nothing about that that's political. This is a public health crisis. And TOMS has stepped in to support."

Amy also has a perspective on which should come first—the purpose or the profitability: "Authenticity is probably one of our biggest values, right? Ensuring that we're doing the right thing first—and then that it's right for business. And I think that that is where you see the most successful purpose-driven companies. I think when companies are doing it because it's on trend or doing it because it's a bandwagon or they think they might make one more sale? I think the savvy consumer sees right through it, and I don't think it's going to be successful for them. But purpose-driven companies also shouldn't be apologetic about the profit piece of this. That's what makes the engine work. Customers are voting with their wallets."

In keeping with its new approach, TOMS's new slogan is evolving from "One for one" to "Stand for tomorrow" (The word *TOM* actually symbolized "tomorrow" from the very beginning—not the name of some mythical founder named Tom.)

"We started to say, 'Let's explore a little more. Let's see what are the other issues, of course, driven by consumer insights and what we know this next generation of consumer cares about." And so we've chosen some new issue areas that we think we're going to be committed to over the long term."

"One of them is mental health, which has so far way exceeded our expectation of where people's passions are. We'll stay with ending gun violence. We also have a category of equality, which is a broad category for us right now. We're still kind of working through where our people's passions are. But that can mean anything from LGBTQ rights to female empowerment to gender equality. And then homelessness, where that gap is becoming wider and wider as we know in the US here."

Finally, we asked Amy for what advice she would give to other leaders engaged in the business for good space. "The three things I try to do every day [are to] stay hopeful, be humble, and try to understand the human components of all of this. Because I think it's really easy to become overwhelmed with how big some of these issues are. And so the three H's that I have written down and stuck at my desk [have] helped me through most days. I also think the other big one that I just continually try to help my team understand is progress, not perfection. I just think business is moving too fast now for perfect. If you're going for perfect, you're not in the game."

Why We Love This Example: TOMS has consistently shown a willingness to listen, learn, and lead. They have always invested money in ways that were consistent with their values. And perhaps the noblest act is their willingness to change their brand Purpose focus areas and evolve with the times. That's part of being a pioneer—and how they still believe that they can create a path to a better tomorrow that will make the world better and others' journey easier.

Chapter 4

Find Your Allies

Once you've found Purpose, you next must find allies: people and organizations whose Purpose intersects with yours. We look at how brands (with their resources and reach) are partnering with nonprofits (which provide in-depth knowledge and problem-solving skills) and architects of cool (who provide the cultural spotlight and storytelling skills to mobilize millions). We'll provide some insight on how you can build powerful platforms and movements that connect and inspire on a large scale.

In this section, see how Jenifer Willig built a community of allies during her time as CMO of (PRODUCT)[RED]—the social-good juggernaut founded by Bono—and how she's applying what she learned there to her new venture, Whole World Water, which works with hotels to generate profits for clean-water projects around the world. We dive into the world of Greg Propper, cofounder of Propper Daley, as he builds alliances between writers, directors, and artists in Hollywood to drive social attitudinal and behavioral change. And Ryan Cummins, the cofounder of Omaze tells us about how he partners with allies such as J.J. Abrams, Robert Downey Jr., and John Legend to give fans once-in-a-lifetime experiences while raising millions of dollars for causes.

Jenifer Willig

Founder, (PRODUCT)^RED

The idea that brands could make money from supporting causes, and not feel guilty about making a profit, was not always a common one. One of the pivotal moments was the launch of the $(PRODUCT)^{RED}$ (also referred to simply as "(RED)") platform, founded in 2006 by U2 frontman Bono and Bobby Shriver to raise awareness and funds to fight against HIV/AIDs. It trailblazed a new type of cause marketing—one that made it more palatable and easy for brands to get involved. It built a mighty coalition of brands from every category: Nike, Apple, American Express, Coke, Starbucks, Armani, Gap—and even got competing brands (such as Converse and Nike) to set aside their rivalry for the common good.

One person who has a deep understanding of how to work with the right allies is Jenifer Willig, who had a ringside seat at (RED)'s journey as their first chief marketing officer. During Willig's four-year tenure, (RED) succeeded in raising $185 million and became a powerhouse global brand with an active social following of more than 2.5 million advocates. She is now the founder of WRTHY, an award-winning social impact agency and consultancy created by experts in strategy, communications, advocacy, marketing, and policy, as well as one of the cofounders of Whole World Water, a campaign to unite the hospitality and tourism industries to help provide clean and safe water to people around the world.

Friendly, open, and disarmingly honest, Jenifer talks about how she got started. She says, "I spent my career in advertising, I was feeling jaded . . . and in 2007, I got a call from a friend who said, 'They're looking for someone to professionalize (RED).' I was never a volunteer, I worked all the time. I wasn't an AIDS activist at the time, though I've certainly been converted!"

The genius of (RED) was that it allowed cause marketing to get out of the doom and gloom and find a new tonality, which allowed brands not to feel guilty about making money from it. Jenifer explains, "It was something (RED) did, as far as AIDS: not portraying it as it had been shown before, as a death sentence, and showing people that AIDS is a preventable and treatable disease; and that it's about living, not dying. That changed the whole perspective and tone—you could have fun with it, you could be cool and irreverent and quirky . . . all of that stuff that when you have a rock star who has founded the organization, you should be able to embrace."

Jenifer knew the importance of making sure the products (RED) sold "led with the cool." She says, "One of the things we learned was that (RED) couldn't sell a bad product; even in 2006, the idea of buying the scratchy sweater because it did good was not going to work as a sustainable business model. There were a lot of people who came to us where we had to push to get their top-selling product. Some people slapped a (RED) logo on a product that wasn't selling well, and it still wouldn't sell—not because people didn't agree with the issue; they didn't want to buy a bad product! And I think that's the evolution of how smart customers are. People are much smarter than we marketers give them credit for. . . . You can't put lipstick on a pig."

Jenifer is now applying that same learning to the Whole World Water campaign, which she explained to us, saying, "A hotel or restaurant joins the global marketing campaign; we provide all of the collateral. Step two is that they agree to provide still and sparkling water to their guests in beautiful reusable glass bottles (designed by Yves Béhar) that we provide. And step three is they agree to give ten percent of their proceeds from those sales to the Whole World Water fund; one hundred percent of that money is used to fund clean and safe water initiatives around the world."

What makes this different from (RED) is that this is a truly global initiative; Whole World Water has members from all over the world, from the Maldives and Mauritius to Africa, Europe, and the United States. And they allow members to earmark the funds they raise for their local communities, which means the funds aren't going to some anonymous project.

Jenifer's passion for the project comes through loud and clear. "There's a billion people living today without access to clean and safe water; it is truly a global crisis that's happening. We have one hundred members so far and seven projects on the ground. It's a win-win-win-win: they reduce their costs by not selling commercially bottled water, they increase their revenue because the margins are much lower, they're reducing their plastic waste significantly, and collectively we can raise money for clean and safe water initiatives."

Her parting advice to marketers: "Find a way to make an impact that is tied to the business; there is nothing wrong with the way you give back also being tied to your business. There are so many models

Chapter 4: Find Your Allies 93

THERE ARE SO MANY

MODELS OUT THERE,

WHETHER YOU ARE A RETAIL BRAND OR A LUXURY BRAND,

that haven't been thought of as yet.

—JENIFER WILLIG

out there, so many innovative ways to impact the business, whether you are a retail brand or a luxury brand, that haven't been thought of as yet. We can't stick to the way things have been done to impact how quickly the world is changing. Businesspeople bring a really strong perspective to social innovation that hasn't been there before. The nonprofit space is a wonderful space and very necessary, but they aren't businesspeople. The beautiful thing I am seeing is that the nonprofits are looking to hire businesspeople to create models and revenue streams that are going to grow the impact they are having. As marketers or business people, we bring a really unique perspective to solving large social issues."

Why We Love This Example: Jenifer's experience with (RED) led to her finding her own area of passion (clean water), but it also led to her finding a unique model that worked for her particular organizational model. There isn't just a one-size-fits-all approach that works for every brand in every category at every stage of life. So keep searching until you find the model that's right for you and your brand. Do small beta tests to see whether it works before scaling it so the organization has time to adjust and implement any information it learns from the tests.

Greg Propper

Cofounder, Propper Daley

The power of Hollywood to influence public opinion has long been clear: From getting the American public involved in WW2 to countless PSAs warning against the dangers of smoking, drunk driving, teen pregnancy, and the like. But in recent years, nonprofits and public health officials have started taking an even more sophisticated approach, one that goes beyond standard tactics to create measurable, quantifiable social change by harnessing the power of pop culture.

So you're sitting on your couch, binge-watching *Orange Is the New Black* on Netflix. One of the female characters who is in prison has a visit with her baby and the baby's father. As the father and baby leave, the female inmate calls out to the father to make sure he reads, talks, and sings to the baby, warning him that otherwise there may be developmental issues. You didn't know it, but that was the handiwork of Greg Propper, one of the cofounders of Propper Daley, a "social impact agency" that works with culture creators in Hollywood to create positive social change.

Greg has a long history of public service in the political and nonprofit world, from working for the Democratic Congressional Campaign Committee in Washington to serving as managing director for Be the Change. We caught up with him about his journey, which has led him to collaborating with the Clinton Foundation on combating childhood illiteracy, with Bradley Cooper on changing the perception of veterans, and with John Legend on the campaign to end mass incarceration. He talked about some of the dangers facing social entrepreneurs that Be the Change tries to solve.

He says, "There's this concept called the social entrepreneurs' trap: as a social entrepreneur you get so caught up running your organization, managing your staff, managing your board, [and] raising money that these brilliant, disruptive, innovative social entrepreneurs who went into this work to change the world end up spending all of their time trying to run and scale organizations that ultimately are difficult to scale—sometimes at the expense of changing systems. And so Be the Change was meant to be a platform for these social entrepreneurs to come together on issues that [they] were stuck [on] and try and get them on track."

To put it another way—Be the Change was essentially about finding allies who could help you with the back-end infrastructure of running and scaling an organization. Greg says, "It was interesting learning actually with our first campaign. We helped, along with our coalition, get passed a piece of legislation in the first one hundred days of the Obama administration called the Edward M. Kennedy Serve America Act, which authorized the expansion for AmeriCorps from 75,000 to 250,000 people a year, which was the largest expansion of national service in this country since the Great Depression."

Despite this success, Greg realized there were other challenges that came with turning the legislation into action. "But to this day it has not been funded, and part of our insight of that time was we hadn't done a really great job with regards to the public. We had reached the president and editorial boards and NGOs, but we hadn't done a good enough job building public will for this idea of service here. We hadn't popularized or normalized this idea of a year of service as a part of what it means to grow up in this country. So when it came time for members of Congress to appropriate funds, there were not enough young people knocking down their doors. So there was sort of this wake-up call for us that we needed to spend a lot more time on the demand side in addition to the supply side, and we needed to do a better job at essentially culture change."

That was the impetus for Greg to move to Los Angeles and start a new chapter in his life, working to create large-scale social change. He says, "I moved to LA to open our West Coast office for Be the Change, and we started working with a lot of folks in the entertainment industry, a number of high-profile celebrities. And at the time they all were saying the same things. It was 2009 and the economy had collapsed and I think most of these celebrities—like everybody else in the country—wanted to feel like they were doing something that was moving the needle. And I think for many of them, they felt like they were spending a little time here, a little money there, but not actually getting anything done."

Greg talks about how he saw the traditional approach to leveraging celebrity and fame to create social change was in need of an update. "At the time in LA, if you were an A-list celebrity or an

Chapter 4: Find Your Allies   99

artist/influencer, and you wanted to create a measurable outcome-oriented change in the world, you had to either hire a nonprofit advisor, who might tell you how to give your money, or a political advisor who will help you shape policy, or a publicist or a marketing firm, all of whom [have] a role to play. But in reality, oftentimes when you're trying to create measurable outcome-oriented change, that is going to require all of those strategies, right? It's just the way change happens in the world. And so our idea at the time, almost five years ago, was to launch a 'social-impact agency.' To try to create a holistic, strategic, one-stop shop for individuals, organizations, [and] companies who are looking to create measurable outcome-oriented change in the world."

A more discerning and savvy public audience also demanded a new approach that prioritized authenticity and real change, as opposed to surface optics. Greg says, "Yes, I think part of it is a growing understanding in general about sort of the complexities but also the need for serious social change. And so part of it, I think, is an acknowledgment among the entertainment and creative community that they have a responsibility, and also the ability, to create real significant change. But I also think the public is more discerning, and the younger generation in particular is more likely to affiliate themselves or to support brands, individuals, or others who share their values, but [they] are also more able and more likely to see through approaches that are inauthentic. I think there's a sort of accountability that comes with a more discerning public."

Greg talked about the importance of moving the public along a continuum from awareness of an issue to attitudinal change to finally behavioral change. "I think there is a default in the social-change field to go right to awareness or just jump right to tactics, when in reality if you want to create real culture change, I think it requires a requisite level of awareness but also behavior and attitude change," Greg says. "So when we work with our clients, nonprofits, individuals, brands, we lead them to a process where we say, 'Awareness plus attitude change plus behavioral change equals X. Where are you strong? And where do we need to do some work? And then how do we more surgically deploy the assets of culture to help achieve that?'"

He continues, "The issue of obesity, for example: generally people are aware that if you eat poorly you're going to gain weight. But you still eat poorly because of peer pressure, stress, or you live in a food desert. Then it's not about awareness, it is about 'How do we use culture to shift people's behaviors and attitudes?' Smoking was another example, right? We had to be aware that smoking causes cancer before [we could] get people to think it was a bad idea and then actually get them to quit. So a part of what we are trying to think about with our clients is how to use celebrity and culture differently to incentivize attitudes and behavior shifts."

One of Propper Daley's recent successes has been around the issue of ensuring veterans are portrayed in a positive light in popular culture. Greg says, "We ran a veterans campaign for example, called Got Your 6. And we launched last year with an event with [first lady Michelle] Obama and Bradley Cooper, something called 6 Certified, where we are working with writers' rooms for television shows and films, and help[ing] introduce it to real-life veterans. And we're helping them understand that not all veterans are heroes, and not all veterans are broken, but most of them are somewhere in between. And then every year we certify somewhere between six and twenty television and film projects that accurately and reasonably portray veterans. And we do a perception-shift study every year in partnership with a research firm in DC to monitor how the portrayals of film and television actually shift the way that the public is perceiving veterans. How am I as an employer, or as a neighbor, thinking about and perceiving veterans as they are coming out? Am I perceiving them as unemployed? Homeless? Having suffered abuse? Perceiving them as heroes on a pedestal, or am I perceiving them as someone who is a lot like myself? Because we know that if they perceive veterans more positively, they'll be more likely to hire them or likely to help them create a successful life."

Building on the theme of "find your allies," Greg talks about how one of the most powerful strategies was to ensure that like-minded organizations, driven by a common purpose, didn't compete with each other but rather streamlined their approach to drive greater success. "So there's a lot of talk lately about collective impact," he says. "How do you bring together a lot of different organizations, brands, [and] individuals who are working towards similar goals but maybe competing for resources, working independently to get them to align around common goals? And I think two of the things that can incentivize that really well [are] one, celebrity, and two, money. So there's a role for celebrity and entertainment to incentivize collaboration amongst a fragmented field. One of the best examples I think is the Entertainment Industry Foundation, who we work with, and their Stand Up to Cancer campaign. They went to the cancer research field and said, 'What are the barriers that are keeping you from doing your work?' Things like, 'People aren't doing clinical trials fast enough' or, 'They are not sharing information.' They took the idea and went to a bunch of brands and funders and said, 'We are going to raise hundreds of millions of dollars. We are going to do a national telecast every two years with every single celebrity in the world.' And then they went to the field and said, 'If you want access to this money, you have to really follow these things,' right? 'You have to do faster trials, and you're going to share your research,' and they ended up creating this Cancer Dream Team. It's an example of one of the most powerful uses of celebrity and brand and funding to incentivize systemic change and collaboration."

Another approach to "find your allies" that Greg highlights is the sterling work being done by artist and activist John Legend around his particular focus on ending mass incarceration. Greg says, "We get to work with John Legend and [his] Free America campaign. John is brilliant, right? He is so smart about this and how to use his profile.

One of the things that he is trying to do is, he did a listening and learning tour of prisons and [brought] policymakers with him. Once he went to the women's prison in Washington State and brought with him one hundred leaders of the labor movement who have traditionally been somewhat resistant to criminal justice reform. But the facts of a broken criminal justice system for labor are that many of their members or potential members are behind bars, or are members who are working in prisons in substandard conditions. So instead of building a barrier, he said, 'Let's go together,' which is kind of amazing."

And in regard to how brands can get involved, Greg talks about an imaginative partnership between Airbnb and Service Year Alliance. (The Service Year Alliance was the result of the merger between the Franklin Project, ServiceNation, and the Service Year Exchange [SYx], and is a joint venture between Be the Change and the Aspen Institute.) "There's a coalition of organizations focused on national service, called the Service Year Alliance," Greg says. "They have been working with brands; one of the most interesting was that they partnered with Airbnb to offer two weeks of free housing to new members while they look for permanent housing. I thought it was a really interesting example [of] how a relevant company can support an unlikely cause, but also how the company or brands can use what is authentic to them and use their assets in a really interesting and productive way."

Why We Love This Example: The work that Greg and his team do builds powerful coalitions between architects of cool—such as writers, directors, actors, and musicians—and nonprofits such as the Clinton Foundation and Service Year Alliance in ways that can create seismic shifts in popular culture and help drive public opinion. It is a model many organizations, including brands, can learn much from as they find ways to harness the power of pop culture to help solve the world's problems.

Dan Goldenberg, Call of Duty Endowment

Activision Blizzard

Programs honoring veterans often are focused on symbolism, such as creating monuments and naming public parks. However, the Call of Duty Endowment believes that the best way to support veterans is to help ensure they have access to high-quality employment when they return home. Dan Goldenberg, the endowment's executive director, shares how they are using the power of gaming to find allies that have helped them put over 125,000 veterans back to work.

The power of pop culture to do good is rich with examples when it comes to music, films, and TV helping to raise awareness of social issues and also drive active fundraising toward helping solve social and environmental problems. But often overlooked is the world of gaming, which is surprising given what a massive cultural and commercial force it is. Flagship gaming franchises such as Call of Duty: Black Ops can make half a billion dollars on a three-day opening weekend (dwarfing even the biggest Hollywood blockbusters) and go on to make $1 billion over two months. More people watch online gaming videos and live platforms such as Twitch than the combined audiences of HBO, Netflix, and Hulu, and the numbers are increasing exponentially as global audiences come online. And the passionate fanbases of these games are a huge community of allies that can come together to unleash tremendous positive impact.

One of the best examples of "gaming for good" is Activision Blizzard's Call of Duty Endowment, which recently reached a new milestone—it's now helped 125,000 veterans find employment since 2009, in jobs that pay an average of $70,000. The endowment has awarded more than $73 million in grants to date, and Activision has donated $40 million of its own money, much of it coming from in-game purchases by players.

The Call of Duty Endowment was born in 2009 from a conversation between Activision Blizzard CEO Bobby Kotick and former Veterans Administration (VA) Secretary Jim Nicholson. Kotick mentioned that a philanthropic foundation was planning on building a performing arts center on the grounds of the VA facility in West Los Angeles, to which Secretary Nicholson replied: "That's stupid. Our real priorities are finding jobs for veterans and improving their health care. I think if we could redirect people's energies and efforts for job creation, that would be a better use of capital and better for veterans."

Inspired by that insight, the Call of Duty Endowment was founded to provide grants to charities that prepare veterans for high-quality jobs and has a meticulous process for evaluating the highest performing nonprofits that meet its benchmarks. That has led to the endowment's average cost to get a vet a stable job being $618 per vet (versus 1/13th of the cost spent by the government).

Leading the endowment today is Dan Goldenberg, who currently serves as a captain in the US Navy Reserve and brings to the job three decades of active and reserve military service and more than a decade of business experience. Enthusiastic and passionate, he talked about the importance of bringing a level of accountability and precision to the task of social impact.

"It's shocking to me, to be honest with you, how many companies check their business smarts at the door. They think when it comes to charity and philanthropy that if you're applying what made you successful as a business, somehow, you're not 'charitable.' And I'd argue that they are exactly wrong. If you apply what makes you successful in business and you apply it to a social realm where you can really add value, you actually do much more good," he began.

Key to the success of their approach is a philosophy of extreme focus, which he expands upon. "The approach that has made us really different is 'Narrow and Deep,' which means we try to do just a few things really well, better than everyone else. So rather than saying, 'We are going to help veterans as a lot of companies do,' we said, 'No, we are just going to focus on veteran employment and are going to be so narrow, we're even going to rule out other worthy, adjacent areas like spouse employment and mentorship. We are just going to focus on vets and jobs.' The thinking being if we do that, we can gain a deep understanding of what's working, what's not, and actually have some real impact."

Chapter 4: Find Your Allies   107

Beyond the total numbers, another subject Dan is passionate about is high-quality jobs, which is why the average 2018 starting salary for veterans placed by their partners is $70,000 (versus the national median, which is $63,795).

"One of the trends—that you won't hear much talk about, but you will in the time ahead—is underemployment. It's a growing epidemic in our country. The US unemployment rate that we all rely upon as a major economic indicator is based on one question that the census asks every month, which is 'last week did you do ANY work for pay?' So if I am a Reservist or Guardsman, and I drilled last weekend, but I don't have a civilian job, I'm counted as fully employed. If I work five hours a week as a barista? I'm counted as fully employed. If I cut my neighbor's lawn for twenty bucks? I'm seen as fully employed. That's the US unemployment rate. So when you see that number in a gig economy, in a world where people are working two or three jobs and have no benefits, what we see is a lot of underemployment. It hits vets particularly hard; it hits them sixteen percent harder than the nonvets. And one in three veterans is underemployed. So to us it's not just that a vet got a job, it's really important to us that they got a good job," he shared.

One of the biggest allies for Activision are the players in the video game world of Call of Duty. Although their world may be fantasy, the positive impact these players are making in the lives of other Americans through the game is as real as it gets. Often the first in-game purchase a player makes is of a product such as the Call of Duty Salute Pack, which helps raise funds for the endowment. Those who have come into the economy by cause become excellent customers, often buying many multiples in non-cause items.

"Something interesting we've observed is that gamers really care about the cause. The support the endowment has gotten from

Activision and the Call of Duty franchise stems from a deep desire to help veterans, period. But we've seen in-game charitable items bring cause-motivated consumers into the game. That was never the intent, but it's a nice by-product," said Dan.

All of this had a profound impact on Dan himself—as well as the employees of the company. "I have no problem leaping out of bed every morning and coming to work. This is the longest I've ever worked anywhere, and I don't feel restless because the commitment from the company is real, and the people I work with are fantastic. I can't even think of a time when someone said, 'Sorry I don't have enough time' or 'I'm not interested.' Activision Blizzard employees are deeply respectful of and engaged with the cause. There is not a function I can think of in the company—legal, marketing, PR, the developers in the studios, IT, HR, artists, sales—who have not found ways to add real value. It's people coming in and solving specific problems with a super high level of engagement."

Why We Love This Example: By finding their allies in the Call of Duty gaming community to help battle the enemy of veteran unemployment, Activision has successfully harnessed the power of passionate fans to do good. They did that by identifying an issue that both their employees and their fans are passionate about. And by going "narrow and deep" on its chosen impact area, Activision avoids the pitfalls of being spread too thin and has learned to find a solution and stay focused on driving impact. By using the game's power to create more equitable access to employment for veterans, they have made an incredible impact on the lives of veterans. Dan has been able to apply decades of experience to solve a problem affecting a community he is part of and cares deeply about. And for that, we salute him, the employees of Activision, the fans—and those on the front lines, keeping us safe through their service.

Chapter 4: Find Your Allies 109

Chapter 5

Think Citizens, Not Consumers

We believe that when brands think of people only as consumers, they are condemned to have a narrow relationship with them. But when they think of people as citizens, they can suddenly see the range of passions and causes they care about, and spot opportunities for collaboration that will lead to a relationship that is transformational, not transactional.

In this section, we meet the passionate creative director Fernanda Romano, and talk about a life-changing project she created with the paint brand Dulux and hundreds of communities around the world; we meet the "inspiring troublemaker" Ahmen, who works for a non-profit by day and is a rapper by night, blending his gifts for social entrepreneurship and social commentary.

Fernanda Romano

Dulux

When exploring the idea of this new model for marketing, we asked ourselves a question: Is this model only valid in countries with developed economies and more sophisticated customers? The answer is no. In fact, we believe it may be even more valuable in the developing world, which has a disproportionate share of complicated issues (climate change and social inequality, to name two) and also the opportunity to leapfrog old models of thinking and go straight into this new paradigm. One inspiring example is how the paint brand Dulux found a way to energize communities around the world from Capetown to Ho Chi Minh City to Rio.

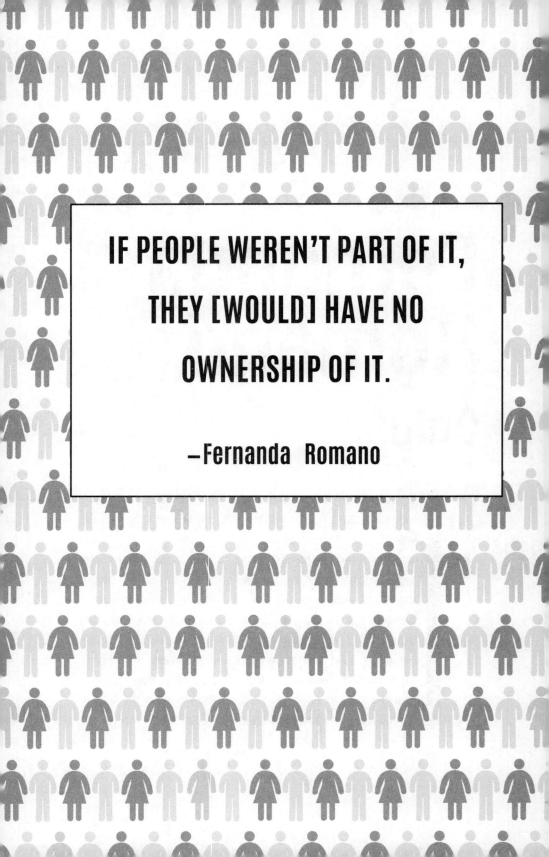

> **IF PEOPLE WEREN'T PART OF IT, THEY [WOULD] HAVE NO OWNERSHIP OF IT.**
>
> —Fernanda Romano

Dulux had a problem. The brand realized they were in a category—paint—that was rapidly becoming commoditized and needed a way to create an emotional connection with its customers. They carried out an intensive program of both internal and external workshops to find out what Dulux and the product it was selling meant to people. And the answer they found was somewhat surprising: color meant emotion. And paint became a way of helping people express those emotions—happiness, optimism, calmness.

Finding their purpose opened a whole new territory for Dulux to explore in their marketing. They realized they had the opportunity to bring color—and optimism—into the lives of their customers. By treating them as citizens and not just consumers, they realized they had an opportunity to engage and collaborate with them in their communities in an unprecedented new way. And so was born the Dulux Let's Colour Project—an open invitation to communities around the world to change gray spaces into colorful environments, done in collaboration with the people living in the neighborhoods themselves.

The very first iteration of the project started in 2010 with four cities in four different countries—the UK, India, Brazil, and France—where in conjunction with hundreds of volunteers (and 6,000 liters of paint), Dulux helped paint schools, streets, squares, and buildings.

Fernanda Romano, who was the creative director at Dulux's ad agency at that time, Euro RSCG (CMO of Supercell, one of the world's leading mobile gaming companies), shared the story of the initiative. Passionate about her craft, Fernanda describes the process by which she got involved and how the project changed her life forever. She says, "The words 'Let's Colour' was the first thing I wrote, the day I came back from the pitch, and then I thought, *This is too obvious*, and I parked it. Then ten days before the final presentation, I went to the planner after we had been struggling for a while to encapsulate it, and he said [of 'Let's Colour'], 'Why did you put it away? That's perfect!'"

Chapter 5: Think Citizens, Not Consumers   115

She continues, "The first thing we presented was a blog, because we wanted to start building a community. We added something crucial: participation. Because if people weren't part of it, they [would] have no ownership of it. So the painting events need[ed] to happen with the community. The brief was finding gray and dull spaces, historical city centers, schools, hospitals, parking lots, places where people come together . . . places that could use a bit of color. [We said,] 'We'll give you the paint, and teach you how to paint, but if you don't paint, there is no deal. And then we're going to document the painting events and turn that into a film, and use that as the invitation to the world.' And it all [came] together with 'Let's Colour' . . . [which] says, 'Come with me and let's do it together.' I get goose bumps just thinking about it."

Dulux turned the process into social media content and documentary films—and even into a two-minute TV spot—which were shared all around the world. The resulting film won a prestigious Ads Worth Spreading award from the TED organization. Hundreds more people started emailing and tweeting at the brand, asking how they could get involved—from everyday citizens in Italy, Chile, Indonesia, and other locations to the governor of Bangkok, who asked them to bring the project to his city.

More recently, Dulux started harnessing the power of pop culture by teaming up with artists and musicians to take the Let's Colour Project to a whole new artistic level. For instance, in the city of Marseille, France, the brand collaborated with mural artist Matt W. Moore, electronic musicians Monsieur Monsieur, and video directors Le Groupuscule to create an amazing video called *Walls Are Dancing*. They transformed city walls with colorful, crazy geometric designs that were then animated into a music video—a gift to the people of Marseille.

When we ask Fernanda what made her the happiest about the Dulux experience, she doesn't even hesitate: "I think what I'm happiest about is that I allowed my work to change me," she says. "In India, I needed to help them because we were losing time, we were in a historic street in Rajasthan, and I was in the middle of the community, and it was so hot, and I took one of the rollers and started, and they came and hugged me and took pictures with me, and I really lived what I was telling other people to live. The paint fell on my head; I spent three hours in the shower, because otherwise I was going to have to shave my head. I have these Chuck Taylors that I wore to every event, and [they have] paint of all colors on them, and I still have them. . . . I was so proud that I wasn't bullshitting people; I was living what I was telling other people to do. I'm really proud of it; it really changed my life."

To date, Dulux has donated around 675,000 liters of paint to projects around the world, with hundreds of events worldwide, from China to Africa to South America and Europe. It has created a groundswell of positive support from citizens around the world.

It also addresses one of key examples of what is known as "cause-washing" or "purpose-washing": touting a noble cause without following through with authenticity. When a company spends $100,000 doing something good but spends $10 million advertising that project, that comes across as fake and inauthentic—advertising masquerading as social good. But if you leave a legacy of a street made beautiful, the positive impact lasts for far longer than an ephemeral TV commercial. It's ROP, not ROI: "return on Purpose," not "return on investment." As Fernanda says, "Your ad is a beautiful street; your out-of-home was the amazing facade of a museum."

Why We Love This Example: Instead of adding to the noise and clutter of people's daily lives by putting up advertising billboards everywhere, Dulux listened to what communities were asking for—a way to brighten up their schools and playgrounds and community centers. And by treating them as involved citizens, not just consumers, Dulux created an army of participants and advocates for the brand. A simple, scalable, colorful idea that could translate to any country around the world.

Eric Dawson

CEO and Christina Rose, CMO, Rivet

Gen Z controls over $3 trillion in annual spending, and they are a completely different kind of consumer. Eighty-four percent of teens screen products based on social impact before they buy, and 62% want brands to have social change initiatives they can participate in. RIVET's CEO Eric Dawson and Chief Marketing & Growth Officer Christina Rose explained how this nonprofit venture enables young people to fund their generation's social impact ideas through everyday purchases.

Young people have been at the forefront of every significant social change movement for the past 150 years, from workers' rights to the Arab Spring. Trailblazers such as Malala Yousafzai and Greta Thunberg have demonstrated how powerful youth-led change can be. Still, they represent only a sliver of the millions of talented, visionary young people across the globe who simply lack the resources to turn their ideas into action. This lack of access to small start-up grants for young social innovators is a systemic issue.

And this is why RIVET was created. It's aligning existing value chains—including brand and consumer power—to rally resources behind young changemakers. RIVET addresses this crucial market gap between consumers and changemakers. Young people trigger corporate donations when they shop with a RIVET brand partner. RIVET turns those funds into micro-grants placed directly into the hands of young innovators through a network of vetted NGO partners.

"We act as a connector, leveraging the existing infrastructure of brands and NGOs to create a flywheel of sustainable funding and scalable impact. Think of us as a mash-up between Bono's (RED) campaign and a microfinance platform like Kiva. We bring together two time-tested models—cause-related marketing and micro-finance—in partnership with a generation that is hungry to act and behind a unique and resonant brand message," Eric shared.

Since its inception, RIVET has been co-designed and co-led by young people who sit in leadership, strategic, and advisory roles both internally and externally. When discussing the long-term potential further, Christina added, "By creating a trusted brand with, by, and for young people, we ignite Gen Z's purchasing power to fuel their collective will to change the world. This youth-to-youth model is infinitely scalable, turnkey for brand partners, and financially self-sustaining. It's also deeply empowering. Whether you are a young consumer shopping your values or a young changemaker improving your community, everyone gets to be a powerful agent for change in the RIVET model."

Prominent brands have joined RIVET as youth allies. RIVET launched a successful pilot partnership with Funko which, to date, has generated four Pops! with Purpose collectibles that sold across e-commerce and retail channels. Each figurine was inspired by the story of a RIVET changemaker and featured popular characters, including Super Woman, Spock, SpongeBob SquarePants and Captain Planet. Also joining RIVET in youth allyship is a group of founding brand partners including eos and Crocs.

Funko will return with a new changemaker-inspired Pops! with Purpose, launched in November 2024. Also joining RIVET in youth allyship is a group of founding brand partners including eos, Fossil Group, and Yoti. Between now and the year's end, RIVET will announce new partnerships exclusively to its online communities and direct shoppers to real-time retail and product opportunities where their purchases help support their generation's social impact goals.

We picked up on the scope of impact that RIVET has created. As of fall 2024, RIVET has funded more than 1,100 youth-led projects in 66 countries worldwide, tackling everything from clean drinking water in Egypt to job creation in rural Colombia. Those projects had an average of five youth leaders for a total of 5,000 youth participants and served an estimated 1,048,230 people in their communities with direct services to improve lives. "We expect to award 10,000 grants in 2024; assuming a similar trajectory, this will mean 50,000 youth leaders directly supported and just over 10 million lives impacted by the youth-led projects. This is powerful, scalable impact," Dawson added.

Remarkably, nearly three-quarters of the young people leading these projects have lived experience with the issue they are trying to solve. Among these young people is Mariana, who founded Rede Autoestima-se to provide free mental health support to marginalized communities in her home country of Brazil after finding a severe lack of affordable psychological resources in her community. Or Walter, who watched the girls in his community in rural Uganda leave school and end their education as soon as they started menstruating. His own sister was married and had four children while she was still a teenager. Walter used his RIVET grant to purchase sewing machines that allow young men and women in the community to produce reusable menstrual pads, allowing girls to stay in school longer and delay marriage and childbearing.

Plans for the future involve potential partnerships with streaming and gaming platforms and payment systems to empower young consumers further to support impactful causes with their transactions. Rose conveyed, "Brand partners are co-identified by our community of youth advisors, ambassadors, and supporters based on the brands they would like to see offering more purchase options that support young people." Key criteria include alignment with RIVET's mission, relevance to young people, and a deep commitment to transparency.

"Our youth community is excited about streaming platforms like Spotify and gaming brands including Epic, Blizzard, Nintendo and EA. Also of special interest are payment platforms that allow young people to turn any transaction into a RIVET purchase and act as a vehicle for recurring donations with each use," she added.

Why We Love This Example: As the young people of the world use their moral imagination to tackle the problems they see, it is heartening to know that platforms such as Rivet have their back—and are helping Gen Z put their money where their mission is. Just as micro-finance revolutionized access to start-up capital for the world's most needy, this "micro-philanthropy" model will drive upward of half a billion dollars into a million new youth-led social innovations over the next decade, created by the most diverse group of young leaders ever.

Justin Parnell

SVP Marketing and Insights, Oreo

When iconic brands take a stand on social issues, they can have enormous impact on our culture. By using their position to champion ideas, they can actually move culture forward in progressive and optimistic new ways. Think about Coca-Cola and "America the Beautiful," which celebrated multiculturalism and diversity. Absolut Vodka championing LGBTQ rights with their iconic "Steve, Will You Marry Me" ad that celebrated marriage equality a decade before it became fashionable. Patagonia announcing "The President Stole Your Land" in the *New York Times*. Nike and Colin Kaepernick. The list goes on. By thinking of its consumers as citizens, Oreo is the latest to blaze a path.

While we would be the first to agree that words must be backed by actions, let us not underestimate the awesome power that advertising alone can have to shape the cultural conversation. A brand that has mastered that has been Oreo (one of our favorite clients at Conspiracy of Love), and one of Gen Z's most loved brands. In fact, in a recent survey of Gen Z, Oreo was the fifth most-loved brand (after Google, Netflix, YouTube, and Amazon, and beating PlayStation, Nike, Instagram, and Nintendo). It makes headlines with jaw-dropping cross-cultural collaborations, whether it's with HBO's *Game of Thrones* or streetwear juggernaut Supreme. Introduced in 1912, it has long been part of America's heritage. The simple ritual of a parent sitting down to have an Oreo and a glass of milk with their child is now as American as apple pie.

It's also been a brand that has been hugely creative on social media, winning it many legions of fans (a staggering 43 million on Facebook alone). When Oreo speaks, people listen. Which is why it has been so impressive to see the brand use its position to champion and celebrate social progress and the LGBTQIA+ community, despite the backlash it generates. We caught up with Justin Parnell, SVP Marketing and Insights at Mondelēz International, to hear more about the journey the brand has taken.

Justin related how he had long dreamed of working on Oreo. "I joined Kraft Foods out of business school and before Mondelēz International came into being. My first assignment was on a tiny little business, Kraft Pasta Salads, and I dreamed at the time of one day leading OREO, our largest global brand. Over the years I worked up the ranks at Kraft then at Mondelēz International across various brand, innovation, and global assignments which ultimately led to where I am today leading the commercial business, marketing and innovation for OREO. I feel blessed to work on such an iconic brand that plays such a meaningful role in people's lives."

He shared his perspective on Oreo's deep heritage around playfulness—and the role it has to play in moving society forward. "OREO is a brand that has brought families and communities together through playful moments for over a hundred years. Playfulness opens our hearts and minds to one another to create deeper connections and acceptance, and it is born out of our unique product experience. OREO is the only cookie that begs to be played with, and is rooted in our classic ritual of twist, lick, and dunk. While everyone has their own OREO eating ritual today, it's the shared experience and love for the brand that brings us closer."

He continued, "What's special is how we activate playfulness in a way that connects with culture and especially the Gen Z audience. On one hand, we play with the cookie to spark playful conversation through collaborations like *Game of Thrones* and Supreme Limited editions. On the other hand, we have really leaned into our values of inclusivity and acceptance, which happen to be very important to Gen Z as well."

As Gen Z is the most diverse and liberated generation in history (in 2024, more than one in five Gen Z adults, ranging in age from 18 to 26 in 2023, identify as LGBTQ+), the brand understands that recognizing and celebrating identity is important. Oreo made its first foray into purpose back in 2012 when they showed their support for the LGBTQ community on Pride Day with a simple social post—an image of the iconic cookie with rainbow-colored creme and the message "Proudly support love!"

Justin revealed, "That was at a time when the US was much more divided on gay rights and it was at the height of the debate around the legalization of gay marriage. It also was not common at that time for brands to step out and show their support. That simple post sparked a maelstrom of controversy, from the harshest critics declaring a boycott on our products to the most passionate fans expressing their love and support."

Justin pays tribute to the marketers who came before him who paved the way. "It's important to share that because it was the defining moment for us as a brand and possibly one that impacted the industry at large. The brave marketers who made that call helped set the stage for us today to live our purpose with conviction. In that regard, I don't take my role lightly for the influence I might have over future OREO brand leaders, who will continue to take the brand to new heights."

In 2019, Oreo made some waves when it decided to do limited edition pronoun packs at Pride in New York City, which said "Share Your Pronouns With Pride," in a nod to the transgender community. The packs (in blue, pink, and purple packaging in a nod to the transgender flag) had "she/her," "he/him," and "they/them" on them. In the transgender community, the importance of being able to choose your own pronoun cannot be overstated: by doing this Oreo signaled a deep respect and empathy.

The accompanying social media post said "We're proud to celebrate inclusivity for all gender expressions and identities . . . encouraging everyone to share their pronouns with pride today and every day." The reaction was immediate on social media. "My beautiful ten-year-old trans daughter who has forever been a fan of Oreo, would love a pack!" said one proud mom. "I love this! Time to hit the market and stock up on massive amounts of Oreos . . . Forever a supporter," said another. "Thank you, OREO!" another replied. "Representation matters. Normalizing asking what a person's preferred pronouns are matters. It's just plain human decency."

But equally swift was the visceral reaction against it. "And this is why I'm glad that my diet doesn't allow your cookies. You've lost a customer. Get woke, go broke," said one poster. "Nabisco thinks it's smart to cater to 4% of the population while disgusting many more," said another. "I wont stop eating Oreos but would never purchase the packaging. Only 2 genders folks. Will always only scientifically be 2. Biology matters!" Conservative groups were outraged and right-wing media lit up at this supposed desecration of an American icon. The outpouring of dismay and disgust at this stance revealed how deeply divided America still is on the issue of transgender identity.

It also revealed the deeper truth that sometimes Purpose is in the eye of the beholder; one person's joyful expression of values is a transgression of another's deeply held religious beliefs or social mores. Justin shared the internal journey to that moment within Mondelēz, the parent company for Oreo. "When it came to the decision on pronoun packs, there was nothing but support across the organization. It was a natural way for us to continue to show our support for the LGBTQ community. We always ask ourselves how we can use our platform to support the issues that matter most to the community. One of those important issues today is to create broader awareness around the importance of pronouns. It was a simple idea—to celebrate inclusivity for all gender identities and expressions. First and foremost, it was to inspire individuals to share their pronouns with pride and also for others to understand the importance of using the correct pronouns as it is one of the most basic ways to show your respect for an individual."

It's important at this stage to note that Mondelēz as a parent company itself is ranked 100 (the highest score) on the Human Rights Campaign's 2020 Corporate Equality Index, for its policies on workforce protections, inclusive benefits, and supporting an inclusive culture. Justin said, "Here in North America, we also have employee resource groups, such as our Rainbow Council, which is focused on building an open and inclusive environment at Mondelēz International for LGBTQ+ employees."

Despite the backlash over the pronoun packs, Oreo went even further in 2020. In celebration of LGBTQ+ History Month, Oreo created a *#ProudParent* platform and partnered with PFLAG (one of the country's leading gay rights organizations, whose name is an acronym for "Parents, Families, and Friends of Lesbians and Gays"). Oreo debuted a new film, titled *Proud Parent*, and released first-of-their-kind Limited Edition #ProudParent OREO Rainbow Cookies to reward acts of allyship for the LGBTQ+ community.

Justin shared the thinking behind the partnership. "Our ambition this year was to go from showing support to truly making a difference. It was about driving the change we want to see in the world—fostering a more loving and accepting world. What we heard from our fans in the LGBTQ+ community is that feeling accepted starts at home. They often fear that the most important bond in their lives, that with their parents, is at risk of breaking when they come out. However, when parents express their love and support it opens the door for greater self-acceptance. That inspired the idea of the #ProudParents campaign which encourages parents to come out in loud public support of their LGBTQ+ children, and has since expanded to celebrate allyship in all forms. PFLAG was the perfect partner as the country's leading ally organization committed to fostering greater LGBTQ+ acceptance."

The film itself is a beautiful and moving piece that shows a real-life couple, Jen and Amy, coming home to what they believe is a disapproving family member—only to see the love and acceptance revealed in the closing moments. We challenge you to watch it without tearing up.

Justin shared more insights about the thinking behind the film. "The film addresses the journey that many parents face after their child comes out of the closet. It shows the love between Jen and Amy, who are a real couple, and the challenges of bringing a partner home for the first time—especially for LGBTQ+ folks. Through the key campaign message, "A loving world starts with a loving home," the film aims to highlight the important role parental and community support plays in fostering greater LGBTQ+ acceptance. We hope this film is relatable to families of all kinds and, combined with the other elements of the #ProudParent program, inspires a new generation of proud parents and allies to come out in loud, public support of their LGBTQ+ loved ones."

As hard as it is to imagine someone being upset at this innocuous and loving idea, inevitably there was a backlash, with conservative outrage group One Million Moms demanding a boycott of Oreo and ranting that Oreo was "airing a gay pride commercial which has absolutely nothing to do with selling cookies" and "normalize[s] the LGBTQ lifestyle" and "brainwash[es] children and adults alike by desensitizing audiences" (Marr 2020).

The tactic backfired spectacularly, with One Million Moms's social media feeds flooded with posts showing loving gay couples—and comments such as "One Million Moms, I just bought a bag of Oreo's and donated to the Trevor Project (another fantastic LGBTQIA+ organization) in your name."

In closing, Justin also shared his personal feelings on how proud he is of this work and the impact that it has had on the wider Mondelēz community. "The stories have poured in from suppliers, customers, employees, friends and family. In fact, it's had an unexpected and very personal impact on me. When I shared the video with one of my closest family members, she was in tears and revealed for the first time to me that she is a mother of an LGBTQ+ child and how hard it is. She told me 'they seek signs of being loved at all times from their family because the world isn't always as kind.' That hit home more than anything and reinforced the responsibility we have as brands to make a positive societal impact. It has been amazing to work on [a] campaign that has had such a profound impact on so many people."

Why We Love This Example: It would have been very easy for this iconic global brand to shy away from controversy and just stick to creating fun and exciting campaigns. But by deliberately choosing to spend its cultural capital on advancing social causes, several generations of Oreo marketers have passed the baton to each other, to help celebrate ideas in society that move us forward in a loving and compassionate way. They understand that this comes with controversy and backlash and the loss of some fans. But by choosing to embrace what the majority of their fans thought as citizens, they placed the brand firmly on the right side of history—giving its many fans reasons to love it even more for generations to come.

Chapter 6

Lead with the Cool, But Bake in the Good

Today it is no longer enough for a brand just to be good; it must also be cool. A new generation of customers is demanding more social consciousness from the brands it buys; but it also wants to make sure that social consciousness is balanced out by the right design, the right aesthetic, the right story told in an authentic and meaningful way.

In this section, we meet Jason Mayden, the inspiring director of design at Jordan Brand at Nike, and talk to him about how designers have a golden opportunity to design not just products but organizations in a way that is diverse and cool. We meet the multitalented Mimi Valdés, the chief creative officer for superstar Pharrell's i am OTHER, who talks about how she's using her skills as a storyteller to make the world a more positive, inclusive place. And then we meet Jocelyn Cooper, the cofounder of the music festival and cultural platform Afropunk, and talk to her about how she's creating a movement that reflects the new America—more racially, sexually, and gender diverse than ever before.

Jason Mayden

Chief Design Officer, Jordan Brand, Nike

Jason Mayden is a designer on a mission. In Silicon Valley, a space renowned for innovation and entrepreneurship, Jason is looking to disrupt the Valley's homogenous status quo by applying his exceptional design talents beyond just physical products, to more boldly apply them to culture—the "first product of any organization"—and in the process make organizations more inclusive, diverse, and accessible to talent previously ignored and undervalued by the tech world.

Before making the move to Silicon Valley, Jason was widely respected among sneaker enthusiasts for his stellar design work with the culturally iconic Nike and Jordan brands. We first were introduced to Jason's story by listening to him speak to a room filled with aspiring footwear designers in Los Angeles at an event hosted by career curriculum platform Behind the Hustle. What struck us most while listening to Jason was his generosity of knowledge and spirit. Although he could have easily played the role of the ultimate cool kid every sneakerhead in the room wanted to be around, he instead shared his experiences with humility and a sincere desire to help each of them create a path to success in business.

Positioned in the front of the room, he stands more than six feet tall, with brown skin, a big smile, and, as he jokes, a perfect round head for the bald look that he pulls off almost as well as his former boss Michael Jordan. He shares his journey of growing up as a kid from the South Side of Chicago drawing sketches of Jordan sneakers for fun to realizing his dream of working for Jordan as the brand's first intern, ultimately becoming its senior global design director, and today serving as the Jordan Brand's chief design officer.

On that day, his stories and advice at the Behind the Hustle event were real, relatable, and moving; and it was clear that his presence that day and the work he chooses to do are all part of a greater calling.

Passionate and purposeful, he spoke of his new roles with the clarity and energy of someone who once boldly proclaimed he wants to "be faster than the future." Jason tells us, "At Accel Partners [a venture capital firm] I helped to amplify and deepen the value and overall impact of design of things within companies, whether they are in the early stage or growth stage of companies. At Stanford [as a media designer/lecturer at the Hasso Plattner Institute of Design], I helped to create moments of critical discourse that allow for true cultural exchange, with the sole intent of providing exposure for these students that are often forgotten about."

He speaks about the common thread between these ventures and why they are so aligned with his sense of purpose in this moment in time. "The thing that ties all of them together is this mindset that what I do is not about me. What I do is to serve other people, using my gifts and talents to help them get the most out of their opportunity. I feel like God has designed me for many things at different times. In this season of my life, my 'why' is to be a counternarrative to what people think is accessible, in the tech industry and the other industries I am in, education and entrepreneurship."

Silicon Valley's problems with lack of diversity in ethnicity and gender have been well documented. Jason strongly believes diversity, inclusion, and exposure—in all forms—lead to greater innovation and better entrepreneurs and founders. As a result, he is looking to help create more inclusive organizational cultures in which all people feel free to be their most authentic selves. "You know a lot of my contemporaries go through this very interesting experience of what I call 'cultural sanitization,' where they want to be included so much in the masses that they are willing to forfeit the very thing that makes them unique and desirable in the first place," Jason says. "My mission is to be myself authentically and hopefully inspire other people to find their own voice and create their own language that defines them, and not join someone else's lane.

"I like to tell people that the mindset of an innovator is to solve the biggest problem that helps the most people. The biggest problem is that we put up barriers as to what we think is cool or as to what we think is smart or intelligent or valuable. And I just want to stand in opposition [to that] and just be myself. Unapologetically be myself and say: 'If you don't think I'm cool or worthy, that's okay. That's your opinion. But I feel like there is a lane of people that will appreciate my perspective and will find courage and strength in me standing against trying to fit in. Because I don't want to fit in if, to fit in, I have to forfeit who I am.' I was just raised to believe that you can play the game, but you don't have to play yourself."

Jason believes part of the problem is the narrow images people associate with designers that leave many talented people feeling like outsiders. He says, "This may sound very controversial, but I would like to see the archetype of design not be a white British male. That, to me, is a falsehood. When I go to look at anything that is design driven, there is usually a white male with a British accent or a derivative of a British accent. While that's cool, I think that's also very defeating for anyone that's a minority, because it's like, 'I don't sound like Jony Ive, or if I don't look like the founder of Dyson vacuum[s], or if I don't look like Marc Newson. But if I don't look or feel like these people how do I find a job that will think I am valuable?'"

He continues, "That to me is the image that we celebrate, and for design, it is very limiting; it's very Eurocentric, and it's usually the same types of people. And I think that's very hurtful for our industry, because we're supposed to be the industry of inclusiveness; we're the equivalent of sports. Where if you have the talent, if you do real work, you should be able to succeed by designing. It's a meritocracy. It should be about the work. Not about the accent, not about the pedigree, just about the work—because it really comes down to that issue.

"But yet we're still struggling with the archetypal images that are put out there, stating [that if] you're not of European descent and not, you know, you don't wear all black, you don't attend fashion week, you don't have an accent, [then] you're not a designer. But I think that is an absolute lie. Because to say that eliminates every single culture that has contributed to what we now call design, particularly the African culture that has created more things than any other culture on this planet, because of our historical advantage. And then second to the African culture ... is the Asian culture, and their contributions. It's fascinating to see how very deliberately our industry has only celebrated European contributions in art and design, when a lot of these concepts are borrowed or literally taken from other cultures.

"So I think that's the big shift: celebrating the contributions from all people to the creative arts, not just some people. Because I see so many students that say they've never met a Black designer, and I'm like, 'Half the stuff you're wearing is made by Black designers.' So half the stuff you read or all these examples or technology to be used—there's some person of color that has been involved. But the outer perception is that we are nowhere to be found.

"In the culture that I live in now, which is an achievement culture, a culture of collective courage, certain people are inspired to speak up and others are told to stick within this lane. Here I am carving out my own narrative, my own unique path, coming from a very different background. That gives me a little bit of confidence to speak up about what I believe is hurtful for innovation, which is the mindset that we all have to be alike in order to succeed in this industry. I think that the moment I am in [Silicon] Valley, with the topic being about race and inclusion, for me, I think that my contribution in this conversation can go far beyond my skin color and my upbringing."

Jason believes the key is exposure. "You know a lot of what I do is behind the scenes. I am a big fan of exposure. A lot of people are fans of opportunity. But for the minority demographic that is being heavily targeted now by tech, they think the way you solve these issues is to say, 'Hey, let's find talented people and give them jobs because they can't fend for themselves, and we have to feed them.' I don't believe that to be true. What they need is the exposure and understanding and a lot of times acknowledgment that they are doing a lot of what is being done here [in Silicon Valley], but it's a different vocabulary.

"So, what I try to do is to create these moments of exposure for young people of color, or for women or any other minority group, to realize that they already have what it takes to be here. They just don't have the vocabulary. No one's told them that if they are out in New York and they have their own small businesses and they are hustling handmade shirts that they are an entrepreneur. They just think they are hustling. But that's entrepreneurship, that's building a business, that is understanding consumer needs, that's demand planning, that's cost saving, that's inventory, that's accounting, that's brand management. It's everything you need to be a founder [of a company].

"But because we've allowed this generation to be conditioned to be consumers, now we are trying to undo that by . . . saying, 'You know what? We want to give you a job at our company. Because if you work at our company, now you're special.' But my mindset [is], we need to give them the tools and the courage to start their own company, to start their own businesses, because in the future the problems are prevented because the founders are already embedded in the concepts of inclusion and diversity, because they come from diverse backgrounds."

Jason is creating opportunities for various communities to gain exposure to the inner workings of Silicon Valley. He speaks about the transformational effect it has on the young people in particular. "As an example, I took about 110 young students from varying socioeconomic backgrounds—primarily African American and Latino—to Y Combinator, which is an accelerator here [in Silicon Valley] for start-ups. This is the first time this group of students, ranging from middle school to graduate school, [has] ever been in this place, [has] ever felt accepted in this place. And they heard for the first time that the vocabulary that they use is valuable to this industry.

"And just the mindset shift in the room was amazing, because my whole thesis is around exposure shifts. Not internships, not access, just exposure. Just provide people with different examples of success and show them that it's possible, and they will step up to the plate, because people become what you expect of them. And right now, they set the expectation that 'minority' means 'needing a significant amount of training.' No, they don't. I mean, we know how to use technology because we consume most of it. We spend most of our money. We spend most of our time. We know how to use it. And we already know how to manipulate it to get the most out of it. But what we don't have is exposure to what it looks like on a daily basis on the creation side. We only have exposure to the consumption side."

Jason is very comfortable with his work mainly being behind the scenes. He is not doing this for attention or fame; rather, he is driven by a deep commitment to expose diverse communities to the opportunities and resources that they need to be successful entrepreneurs. "So every single thing that I do is not intended to make it to the media. It is intended to give the confidence and self-efficacy that is missing from this generation in minority talent. The ability to feel like they can do it and they have a safety net. Like most of the entrepreneurs who are successful, here are people who don't talk about it because they come from wealthy families and have a safety net. So, they can take greater risks, but minorities, historically we only know risks. We only know sacrifice. We only know struggling. So we are predisposed to being great founders, because we have to live scrappy for generations. So the mindset of being lean and being scrappy is not a unique concept to minorities. What is a new concept is the idea that that translates to being the founder of the company.

"So that's all . . . I'm trying to do: build a bridge back to where I've come from, the neighborhood I've come from, the mindset that I used to have, [from] the mindset and neighborhood that I'm living in now. And just tell them that, 'Yo, you can completely be yourself. Use all of the things that you've learned growing up in NY,

Chicago, LA, Houston, Medici, Tokyo, India to become something special and something that is real and authentic."

In these inner-city neighborhoods, Jason believes there is a wealth of untapped talent that can be the new founders of the next wave of successful companies. Talented, driven young people already equipped with the qualities venture capital firms such as Accel are looking for but who lack the exposure Jason sees as essential. He describes this group in an essay he penned titled "The Rise of the Cultural Alchemist," a term he defines thus:

"A 'Cultural Alchemist' can be defined as 14–25 years old, contextually educated, multiracial, methodically creative, socially aware, culturally blended and technologically proficient. They are driven by genuine interactions, exchanges of ideas, collective aspirations and access to experiences that lead to meaningful opportunities. They are not just looking for a job, they are looking for a mission and a purpose. They are the champions of the future. They do not believe in 'picking a lane.' They believe that they are the lane."

Jason is now "working to inspire and create access to opportunities for the emergent Cultural Alchemists of the world," who he believes "will define the way we live, work, play, interact, and dream." As Jason continues to redesign organizational cultures in ways that enhance innovation and expand entrepreneurship, he thinks in the future more designers will play driving roles in creating places where inclusiveness and exposure in all forms are leading to great design. He says, "You know, I think there will be more of a shift to designers who can become chief culture officers for companies. I think designers are going to radically change the way that human resource departments are created within the organization; if companies are forward-thinking and really understanding that the first product you create is your culture, and the first consumer is your employee base. I think that's how we're going to build better companies, better corporations, better governments, and better societies," Jason says.

The first product you create is your **culture,** and the first consumer is your **employee base.**

— Jason Mayden

"By bringing the mindset of human-centeredness into every discussion, not just when it comes to making a machine or making an app, but in building these organisms that we call organizations. So that, to me, is the future, and not like the distant future; it's in the next two, three years.

"Because when the millennials . . . you know, I'm at the beginning of the millennial era, where children born in the 1980s . . . there is no way that you can just throw money at us and keep us loyal. You have to be solving problems that we find interesting and relevant. You have to be a culture that is flexible and dynamic. You have to be willing to allow us to work in the way that we feel comfortable; meaning we may want to work from home, we may want to work on an airplane traveling somewhere, we may want to work at an office. But you have to be more fluid, not rigid. And those are all design problems, but design schools, they don't think about those jobs. So I would say that's what I'm seeing; that's what I am interested about. The further I get into this, in my current career, I feel like I am being pulled into being one of those people who helps create culture in companies. And it's fascinating, because I went to school to make product, and now I'm being asked to help create cultures, which is so interesting to see the shifts, you know."

Why We Love This Example: We love the notion that culture is the most important product organizations create, that employees are the first customers, and that by designing inclusive cultures where employees are able to be and contribute their most authentic selves, you can bake in the good in a powerful way.

Mimi Valdés

Chief Creative Officer, i am OTHER

i am OTHER, the creative umbrella for all of Pharrell Williams's ventures, knows exactly what it stands for: individuality, the uniqueness and diversity that make us all valuable and beautiful. Mimi Valdés, its chief creative officer, shares how they embed that DNA in every story they tell across fashion, film, music, and beyond to create a world where everyone sees the beauty in each OTHER.

It is a beautiful summer day, the kind of perfect weather you dream about during the long winter months. The energy seemingly everywhere in the city is vibrant and upbeat, making it almost impossible to have a bad day, even if you wanted to. A newly washed SUV drives through the busy traffic blasting the hit song "Happy" by Pharrell Williams, which feels like the perfect soundtrack for today's mood. Teens are outside, lined up on the sidewalk waiting to see the new coming-of-age film *Dope*.

The line of teens looks like a modern-day Benetton ad, where seemingly every possible ethnic group imaginable is represented and harmoniously interacting. They are all dressed in their freshest summer fashion; one kid has a hat nonchalantly turned backward as he tries his best to charm the petite Hispanic girl he has his sights on. His hat reads THE SAME IS LAME, and a quick glance at the line of footwear on display suggests that may be a mantra for this group. At least a dozen of the teens are in some different shade of a seemingly never-ending pantone of colored Adidas shell toes.

There is clearly a shared ethos among this group—individuality, creativity, coolness, and optimism—that connects them to each other and to a single brand, i am OTHER, which is the creator of the music in the streets, the clothing they are wearing from head to toe, and the movie they are waiting to see. We took a deeper look at i am OTHER and how the beauty of individuality is the purpose that links all their endeavors in fashion, film, and music.

i am OTHER is the umbrella brand for all the creative ventures for music superstar and cultural pied piper Pharrell Williams, and while every one of these cool kids knows Pharrell, it is Mimi Valdés, his creative partner and i am OTHER's chief creative officer, who is a driving force in bringing this colorful, diverse world to life.

Summer days like this should feel familiar to Mimi, who grew up in New York, one of the most multicultural cities on the planet.

She is used to seeing millions of people of every shade, gender, faith, and orientation, and knows each of them has a story to tell.

She is smart, confident, and connects with a genuine warmth and infectious youthful energy. As a journalist, she has told the stories of some of the biggest names in popular culture, and now as a chief creative officer, she is helping to inspire millions of others to celebrate their individuality through narratives across film, television, music, and products.

From a young age, Mimi was interested in learning about and telling stories, and so it makes sense that a natural storyteller born in the most eclectic city in the world would grow up to tell stories that capture and celebrate the unique diversity we all share. She says, "Being born and raised in New York City, in Manhattan, I went to school with everybody, right? When I walked down the street, I saw everybody. To me it is weird when you are in places where there aren't different kinds of people. So of course I have my eye out and heart in diversity, real diversity.

"I felt from a very young age that I was meant to tell stories. I was always attracted to it. I think in my head I am always first of all a journalist, always and forever, and I love good stories. I love stories that haven't been told before but yet are super relatable to people—just everyone, regardless of what your color, race, ethnicity, [or] sexual orientation is. Those are the kind of stories that I am always attracted to. I can't remember a moment of being like, 'OK, I want to tell stories,' but that was what I always felt like I was supposed to do, and then as time has gone on, it changes to different things. Right, it was working for magazines or websites or coming to work with Pharrell."

One of Mimi's first jobs after graduating from NYU was working at *Vibe*, an upstart magazine founded by Quincy Jones, which would grow to become one of the most authoritative and influential voices in youth culture. Starting as an intern, Mimi rose through the ranks to become editor in chief. She tells us, "When I became editor in chief of *Vibe*, I was the fourth or fifth one, and I remember thinking at the time—because I am a crazy Virgo that's always analyzing things—*OK, what's next after this? There is a possibility that this might not last forever*. But I wasn't sure what that [next step] would be, but I just remember thinking, *Just make sure you do a really, really good job. You have your relationships, and make sure that you cultivate them and cultivate them in a way that people aren't just dealing with you because you're the editor in chief of* Vibe."

Those Virgo instincts proved again to be valuable when *Vibe* was sold to a private equity company, which resulted in massive layoffs. Mimi says, "I remember when everything happened at *Vibe* I got phone calls from Jay Z and all these artists [who] reached out on some, like, 'Are you good? Are you OK?' [level]. And I remember saying, 'Aw, man! So people didn't deal with me just because I was editor in chief of *Vibe*. They honestly care about me, actually really are concerned that I am good.' And I felt proud about that, because I was like, *The important thing is, if you do a really good job, you'll figure it out*.

"So after that I went to *Latina* magazine, I was there for a while, became editor in chief there too. After that I was VP of digital content at BET.com."

Although the BET job didn't work out as she planned, it led her to i am OTHER with Pharrell, an opportunity that would unleash her creativity and purpose in ways beyond what she could have imagined. Given their friendship and kindred values, it was a perfect fit.

"Pharrell and I, you know, are friends for a reason; he is like my little brother," Mimi says. "We look at the world the same way, we share a lot of the same values and approaches to just life in general, so when it came time to start i am OTHER—he calls it a creative collective, and it's really the umbrella company for all of his ventures—he was just like, 'Come on board.' So I decided to quit."

Together, they began building the brand the way these authors believe all successful brands should be built: by starting with a clear understanding of what you stand for and the impact you want to make in the world. That collaborative process began with looking back at the core values that inspired Pharrell's music production and recording collaboration N*E*R*D, and identifying the core values they felt needed to be embedded in i am OTHER.

Mimi says, "The thing we thought about—just like what he did when he first came out with N*E*R*D—the reason why he made it, he wanted to somehow make being a nerd cooler, education cooler, being smart cool; that was the goal. So much so that when Shepard Fairey, who designed the HOPE poster for Obama, designed that N*E*R*D logo, the brain, it came from him being like, 'The brain represents education.' He's always wanted to promote that, and when it came time for i am OTHER, it was those same values. I always believed individuality is something that people should be proud of."

She continues, "And OTHER—the name of the company— actually came from Lauryn Hill, strangely enough. Years ago, when [Pharrell] was about to work for her, she told him, "I like what you guys do. You're different; but when you work with me, I need other,' and Pharrell was like, 'Oh my God! Other!' That always [stuck] in his head, so when it came time to revamp his company and he wanted a fresh start to look at stuff, the idea of otherness, that stood [out] in his head."

Whereas most brands bury their values and purpose in HR folders or on plaques in the corporate hallways, i am OTHER made it a point to proclaim theirs for the world to see, giving everyone a clear understanding of what they stand for and the principles that guide their community and everything they create. For example, Mimi says, "On the website, there's a manifesto of what 'other' is, and the importance of individuality and experiences being the new wealth. That came from wanting to explain the mentality, what it is and how we approach every project. So it's like everything is part of wanting to spread that idea of why individuality is a cool thing. Obviously, the world has changed, but we still have numbers of people being attacked or shunned or something because they are different. And we're like, 'Man, you are crazy. You are looking at the world in really not the right way,' because the beauty of this world is the fact that we are so different and we have different experiences and different lives, but at the same time there is a commonality and a desire to just do good and do good work that feels good.''

Mimi shares how the importance of individuality shapes her current role. "As chief creative officer, I oversee all of our creative endeavors. With our film and TV stuff, I am his producing partner. We do everything together. I go out there and basically try to find projects—movie projects—that make sense for us, for me, for him, for the brand. The great thing about someone like Pharrell—whose main job is music—is when he's doing film and TV, it's awesome in the sense that there is not a lot of pressure to just get a bunch of projects going. We can be very selective. While it is an important part of the company to concentrate on, we don't have this sort of bottom line where we are like, 'We have to do X amount of movie projects a year, we have to do X amount to TV projects a year.' It's like, if it makes sense, we'll do it."

When asked about what filters guide the partnership process, she says, "I think it's really all gut, as silly as it sounds. It's not really about any kind of market research or algorithms or how successful a brand is. All those things, they freak Pharrell out, they freak me out; that is not how we make decisions. Both Pharrell and I . . . the way we approach work is, 'Does this feel good?' Then this must be the right thing that we are doing.' Because it feels good regardless [of] whether it's successful or not, [and] that's a win for us. And that is really a blessing, especially for someone like me, who is a creative."

Those gut instincts paid off when it was time for Mimi to produce her first music video for Pharrell's hit song "Happy," which became one of the biggest cultural phenomena of the last decade. Her lifelong experience as a storyteller and passion for diversity had prepared her perfectly for this moment. And by baking i am OTHER's core value of celebrating individuality into the concept from the beginning, she was able to help create something that felt authentic and accessible to millions around the world.

Mimi says, "We know what we stand for at i am OTHER; we know we stand for individuality. People expect new ideas from us, things that haven't been done before, but as you know, almost everything has been done before, or that's what it always feels like. But I think the only way to do things that are different is to innovate. And in order to do 'new ideas, or a new spin on ideas,' which is basically the way that we look at the world, there almost has to be a little bit of fear in deciding to do the project; it has to feel kind of risky. For me that always feels like a good place. I always knew that personally when something feels risky, a little crazy, I am like, 'OK, we are on the right path,' because if it doesn't feel that way, then that means it has been done before.

"I had never done a music video before. That was my first time working on a project like that, and it was sort of the same thing. I approached it as a journalist, [but] Pharrell had a different idea of what he wanted to put in that music video. . . . I just remembered in the movie [*Despicable Me 2*] when the lead character, Gru, realizes he is falling in love, he starts dancing, and when 'Happy' plays in the movie, he's dancing down the street in scenes of happiness. I was like, 'That's what you should do! You should do that scene from the movie; we should just sort of replicate that.' But again, that came from a place of good storytelling."

Mimi's intuitions on the concept of the video proved to be spot on, but it was the creative audacity of its execution that made the video so remarkable. Proclaimed as the world's first 24-hour music video, it features an array of people dancing including Pharrell, Magic Johnson, Jamie Foxx, and actress Miranda Cosgrove, in various environments. Fans were able to watch clips across multiple media outlets or view the full video on the main website, which was time stamped to show when people were filmed over a 24-hour period.

"I remember getting the treatment and getting to the page where they had the twenty-four-hour concept, and I remember slamming my computer shut, like, 'Oh my God!' It was like the biggest idea in the world. It felt so crazy to me, and honestly I didn't know how this was going to get done. 'This sounds so crazy and probably impossible, but fuck it! Let's figure this out! If the directors feel confident they can figure it out, I'm just going to go ahead and believe it.' Maybe that was the naïveness, maybe that came from not knowing how all of this would work, but it felt crazy. It felt like, you know, 'I don't know how we are going to do this.' I think a lot of times that's kind of how we approach things."

She continues, "The directors [the Paris-based directing team We Are from LA], they were the ones that came up with the twenty-four-hour concept that this was born out of. You know, the directors were just awesome, but I remember being like, 'This [is] a family movie, so let's have everybody, let's have kids, let's have older people, let's have all shapes and sizes!' Even to the point, I remember telling the casting girl, 'I want different shades of Black people, and not everybody can have a weave. I need, like, natural hair; I need braids!'

"I was so explicit about that because I was like, 'Let's make sure we are representing everybody and making it really, really diverse.' The more people you include in telling the story, then the more chance you have of it reaching as many people as possible.

"But of course, no one knew it would become what it became. It felt good to know that, 'OK, we did this right. We did this in a way that everyone felt included and wanted to participate in it and show that they were also happy too.'"

With the massive success of the "Happy" video, it made sense that the next natural progression would be a film, and so in partnership with writer/director Rick Famuyiwa, as well as producers Forest Whitaker and Nina Yang Bongiovi, Mimi and Pharrell co-produced the movie *Dope*, a coming-of-age film about an African American teenage nerd who, along with his eclectic group of friends, navigates the dangers of a tough LA neighborhood while pursuing his ultimate goal of getting accepted into Harvard University. The film creatively ties together several of the themes i am OTHER celebrates—individuality, education, and openness—into an entertaining film that resonates with many young people who otherwise don't see themselves represented in the stereotypical ethnic imagery of most Hollywood films. As a result, the film has developed a cult following among legions of youth who identify with that sense of otherness.

From the beginning, the film was a critical success, winning rave reviews and multiple bids at Sundance. However, it was the response at Cannes that shocked Mimi, and a conversation with Pharrell that reminded her about what's most important and the impact her work should have in the world.

She says, "We did *Dope*, and we already had the success at Sundance, but we got into Cannes, and I was really shocked. And then we're there at the premiere, and then I started to get really nervous because I knew that when the French come, when they don't like a movie, they boo it. So I was paranoid, and I was like, 'Oh God! Please don't let them boo our movie!' And Pharrell was next to me, and he looks at me and says, 'Calm down!' He was like, 'We are at Cannes, we have a movie here. Who cares? What difference does it make? It's going to be fine; it's going to be fine.' Look where this movie took us. He was like, 'You're looking at this the wrong way, Mimi.'"

Chapter 6: Lead with the Cool, But Bake in the Good   151

She continues, "You know, sometimes you just have to be reminded that it doesn't matter if it's successful or not. Like, did it feel good making it? Was there purpose in it? Can this inspire people in some way? For me, always when I've created any kind of content, told any kind of story, my three rules are I want to educate, I want to entertain, and I want to inspire. If the content that I have worked on [has] those three things, then I am good. Then I feel like I have done my job, because those are three things I think are successful storytelling. But regardless of how big your audience is or how small it is, you can do those three things, and then I think it's a win."

After *Dope*, Mimi expected to build the film and TV division doing indie movies, slowly graduating to studio movies. However, it was a chance meeting that gave her an unexpected opportunity to tell an amazing story that had been waiting more than 50 years to be told. She tells the story of how she and Pharrell became executive producers on the film *Hidden Figures* with Fox 2000 Pictures, coming out in 2017—their second movie and first studio movie.

Mimi explains, "Randomly, I have this meeting with Donna Gigliotti, an Oscar-winning producer. She is from New York, an amazing, amazing woman—she won the Oscar for *Shakespeare in Love*, but she also did *The Reader*, she also did *Silver Linings Playbook*. So this is someone who is like, super-established and has a legendary track record. I had a meeting with her about another project, and so we just start talking and having a really good time, and we both kinda liked each other. And I just happened to ask her what kind of projects she's working on. So she's like, 'Well, you know, I've optioned this book; it hasn't come out yet. It's called *Hidden Figures*. It's about African American women that worked at NASA; they were kind of the human computers. The Black women were called the colored computers, and they hand-calculated some of our space missions, notably John Glenn's first space orbit [on the Mercury-Atlas 6 "Friendship 7" spacecraft],' and I am looking at her like, 'Oh my gosh! Are you serious? One, how do I not know about this? And two, please, please; Pharrell will die when I tell him about this! Can we be involved in the project?'

"I am like, 'We will do anything from music to screening; I'll put you on the phone with Pharrell.' So immediately, the next day, I put her on the phone with Pharrell. Anyway, long story short, we get on this movie, and I couldn't be happier, because then I get to Atlanta and Taraji [P. Henson] plays the lead, named Katherine Johnson. Octavia Spencer plays one of the other women (Dorothy Vaughn); Janelle Monáe plays the other woman (Mary Jackson). Kevin Costner plays the head of the space task force, Kirsten Dunst another key role. So it's just an incredible cast, and one of the most amazing experiences that I've had, simply because it is just a great story, and everybody on set knew the importance of the story. You could just feel it in the energy. They were like, 'OK! We are here because we want to do this movie and these are great roles, but man, this is an important story!'"

The moment made Mimi reflect on her journey and the idea that some things are predestined. She says, "Cheo Hodari Coker is a journalist-turned-screenwriter, and he is a really good friend of mine. He always knew he was going to go into screenwriting; that was his goal. He was always telling me, from the '90s, that I'd be a great producer or writer—'whatever it is you want to do.' I was kind of like, 'Yeah, OK?'

"It seems like a fantasy, but OK. And I remember buying a couple of books at the time, maybe some screenwriting books, some producing books, but I don't think I even read them. I might have just looked through them, and they just kind of sat in my bookshelf. Fast-forward like twenty years later when the *Dope* opportunity came about and I was in LA shooting that. And Cheo hears about it, and he was like, 'I told you! I told you, you was gonna do all that!' And I was like, 'You did! You did tell me!' I said, 'I guess I should have paid attention!' But everything happens for a reason. Everything happens when it's supposed to."

It's clear the universe is letting Mimi know this is the work she is supposed to be doing. "I just want people to recognize that diversity is beautiful, that it's not something to be scared of," Mimi says. "If anything, it's something to seek and to appreciate because you can really color your world in a way that maybe you didn't anticipate, right? It's that childlike wonder that you have in kindergarten that unfortunately I think a lot of people lose as they get older, because they feel like that's not how they should be experiencing the world.

"And it's exciting, because of all these beautiful moments that get captured in your childhood when you are appreciating differences, that's what it is. And for whatever reason, I don't know what happens when you get older and you start to lose that childlike wonder and the appreciation, and that curiosity fades. So for me, I just want to remind people, like, 'Remember that feeling?' Everything you say you were curious about, you should look at diversity in the same way. The more you can be exposed to different people and cultures, whether it's food or different cities or different music[, do it]. What a gift to be able to experience all that diversity, and it can just inform and color who you are, right?

"I don't know if that comes from me being obsessed with stories and storytelling and starting out as a journalism major at NYU, but that dedication to just wanting to learn about the world is something that more people need to just experience. Because it's fun, really fun!"

Why We Love This Example: We love this example because it shows how to harness popular culture to express our purpose in innovative ways. By uniting her personal purpose of telling diverse stories that educate, entertain, and inspire with i am OTHER's creative platform for celebrating individuality, Mimi has been able to tell narratives in creative ways that deeply connect the i am OTHER brand and its offerings with the hearts and minds of people around the world. In the process she reminds us we are all other, and yet we are all one.

154 GOOD IS THE NEW COOL GUIDE TO MEANINGFUL MARKETING

Jocelyn Cooper

Cofounder, Afropunk

"Good Is the New Cool" isn't just an idea that we saw in mainstream pop culture. Some of the most interesting examples we saw came from the very cutting edge, the vanguard, the alternative fringes of society. One such inspiring example is the Afropunk movement, which has created a safe space for "the New America"—more ethnically, sexually, and gender diverse than ever before, where people are free to design their own cultural identities from a wide-ranging palette of influences and choices.

Walking through the fields of Commodore Barry Park in Brooklyn during the annual Afropunk Festival is to see a vision of the future of America. There are people of all ages and colors here, dressed eclectically, letting their individuality shine through in hairstyles, clothing, tattoos, piercings. The vibe is super chill, inclusive, and nonjudgmental. Lesbian couples walk arm in arm, while Black skater kids practice their flips. We watch from the mosh pit as Jada Pinkett Smith launches into a fiery tune with her nu metal band Wicked Wisdom, while her spouse, Will Smith, bobs his head approvingly from behind the soundboard. Then things get even cooler when a three-piece band of young Black teenagers called Unlocking the Truth comes out and absolutely slays the crowd with the tight ferocity of their heavy metal.

The crowd goes wild. Welcome to Afropunk.

The story of Afropunk began with a young entrepreneur named Matthew Morgan, who coproduced a seminal documentary titled *Afropunk* in 2004 that tracked the nascent Black punk rock movement consisting of bands such as Fishbone, Bad Brains, TV on the Radio, and many others. Matthew sought to create screenings to promote the movie, which became mini musical experiences in and of themselves, and ultimately led to the staging of the first Afropunk Festival in 2005. Over the years the festival has blossomed to 60,000 people, and headlining acts have included such artists as D'Angelo, Lauryn Hill, Lenny Kravitz, Body Count, MeShell Ndegeocello, Sharon Jones, Chuck D, Kelis, Gary Clark Jr., and Grace Jones. The common thread? All artists who have blazed their own unique musical path, refusing to be pigeonholed into either mainstream hip-hop or mainstream R&B.

The 2016 lineup included TV on the Radio, Tyler the Creator, Janelle Monae, Flying Lotus, Ice Cube, the Internet, Gallant, Cee-Lo, Fishbone, George Clinton, Living Colour, and Saul Williams—some of the most influential artists performing today, side by side with the legendary artists that have influenced them. It is a testament to Afropunk's rising star that the lineup doesn't just reflect the cutting edge of black culture, but the cutting edge of *American* culture, period. This is the new Harlem Renaissance, coalescing the worlds of music, art, and film into a scene that has now expanded to such diverse threads as the nuanced comedy of duo Key and Peele, contemporary artists like Sanford Biggers and Wangechi Mutu, and filmmakers Ava Du Vernay (*Selma*) and Ryan Coogler (*Creed*). And let's not forget the ultimate stereotype breaker, President Barack Hussein Obama himself.

Matthew's cofounder in Afropunk is Jocelyn Cooper, who has been there since the inception. She talks about how her earliest influences were her parents, especially her father. "Each day my life's work comes from being inspired by my father, who worked for a company called F & M Schaefer Brewing Company, a very famous beer company in the '70s in New York. My father was the community development person and helped shape Schaefer's support of theaters and galleries. He inspired me to do the work that I now do around the idea of using entertainment as a medium and as a powerful form to influence and to 'edutain' [mixing education and entertainment]. That has always been in the forefront of my mind."

Jocelyn has had a checkered career working in the music business at some pivotal moments in culture. She says, "So I worked for record companies and publishing companies, and worked for L.A. Reid. I ran the A&R department at Universal, and I always knew how powerful the 'entertainment' side was. And being able to use that for good versus evil has always been my goal. I'd been sort of involved in transitional cultural points like signing D'Angelo and ushering in neo-soul. Or at Universal, signing and working with Cash Money, helping to usher in the new hip-hop-soul movement and blow that up in a way that it hadn't blown up before. Now [Universal] continue[s] to have their legacy with Drake and Nicki Minaj, and they monopolize hip-hop. So I had seen the power of

WE ARE A PLATFORM FOR

Freedom of Expression

— JOCELYN COOPER

what happens when you have obviously great music, fashion, and culture collide."

Jocelyn's time at the epicenter of popular Black culture helped her realize how it could be used for good—and how it could be exploited. "When I was working for Universal, I was sitting in meetings with folks who weren't necessarily interested in the culture but more in the bottom line," she says. "You have to make decisions on culture and music around what is selling, and sometimes the lowest common denominator . . . and it's heartbreaking. You know, getting back to my family's work at things political and empowering talented people of color; it was really disheartening to be a part of destroying it on some level. I remember a video that came through: two kids, who I can't remember the name of now, and in the video there is a seven- or eight-year-old girl who had on gold shorts, and she was carrying a little boy in a red wagon, and the statement they were making was this little girl was the hoe and the boy was the pimp. I remember saying, 'I actually don't want to be a part of this!' There was no way. My parents would be ashamed."

There was something special about the early days of Afropunk that made her realize that it was different from just another ephemeral music genre or scene. She says, "Afropunk was very different because it was happening on every single level, from fashion to lifestyle to comedy—just across the board there was a cultural shift. And for me that was the most exciting piece of it. I was like, 'This is bigger than hip-hop, this is bigger than anything I've ever seen, because it is happening on a level around history, around identity.' I started to see it with Black kids on skateboards in Brooklyn. The word 'punk' is a word that freaks people out, but then to see the shift where kids were identifying with that as who they are? It's an amazing journey, because it's positive."

As Afropunk evolved from a film to a festival, it became something much larger that encompasses editorial, social media, and

Chapter 6: Lead with the Cool, But Bake in the Good   159

much more. Jocelyn tells us, "I mean, we happen to be a platform for freedom of expression. The festival itself is just a celebration of that. There's this notion that people of color, Black people in particular, are homogenous—there's either the hip-hop box or everyone else. I think what Afropunk has done is opened up the dialogue that there is more than just two groups and a monolithic approach to Blackness; and that is obviously pervasive with the president, and with *Hamilton* . . . but I think Afropunk for young people is how they see themselves. Millions of them. And globally too, as we are taking the festival around the world. We are in Paris, we are in London, next year we'll be in South Africa and Brazil; you see the need for the platform."

This pretty much sums up what Afropunk's ethos is: the home for the alternative Black experience, the one you don't see reflected in mainstream media. It is a beacon for those who have felt disenfranchised by pop culture and who don't feel like they fit into easy categorization based on their race or gender. Jocelyn talks about a couple moments where she realized that something bigger was happening, taking it from a niche scene to something bigger.

She says, "There was a moment at the festival when we went from, I think it was 10,000 people to 30,000 people a day. And that happened in 2012, and we had almost lost everything in 2011 to the hurricane [*Sandy*] . . . it just all just came together in a moment. And for me personally, it was D'Angelo playing Afropunk because I have been on this journey with him since he was seventeen years old, as his publisher. So to see him performing at the festival, and the set that he did at Afropunk where he didn't do any of his music, where he did covers of Fishbone and Sly Stone, the pioneers, the Afropunk originals, with The Roots? That was a magical moment for me personally."

In addition to the 60,000 people at the event, Afropunk has a reach of millions online; they are the ones on the cutting edge of culture, seeking out new art forms and sources of inspiration that speak to their experience. A recent survey of their audience showed that 68% purchased books regularly, 38% had passports, and 40% defined their race as multiethnic. Moreover, 90% of them had "some college" (versus the average of 57% in the general population). But 45% said "brands didn't get them," showing that the opportunity to connect with them still exists. Brands have stepped up, though; Red Bull has been a sponsor, as have others, such as MillerCoors.

Jocelyn talks about what makes for a successful partnership with their community. "Red Bull really has a team of people that really loves the Black culture, and we've been working with them now for four or five years. That's a company that invests in culture long-term. We've worked with them on many things, in particular Red Bull Sound Select, and we've put so many artists through that, everyone from Cakes Da Killa to Unlocking the Truth, Le1f, Princess Nokia, The Skins . . . a list of acts who are starting to resonate, starting to make some noise, that are helping to shift culture in a really positive way [and] that are getting support from that program. . . . When Red Bull invests in something, it usually invests long-term; when you build something with the community, you have got to do it long-term. We've partnered with MillerCoors, who have been amazing. But we haven't had more major brands come on to work with us in that way, but I think we'll get there. We are still fighting and working to get there."

And Afropunk has now found a way to turn the appeal of its festival to spark even more social good. Jocelyn tells us, "We started our nonprofit organization called Afropunk Global Initiative, and 22,000 kids went through that program doing community service in order to earn a ticket into the festival. Those kids did everything from going to community board meetings to making homeless kits for homeless people—kids actually sitting down for an hour talking to a homeless person about what's going on with them. And that kind of work, which is supported by the mayor's office in New York and Art for Amnesty with Amnesty International, is really important."

Afropunk's culture of inclusiveness and tolerance has even greater resonance today, with its ability to create safe experiences for young kids under attack. "We just came back from our show in Atlanta, where seventy percent of the audience was LGBTQ kids, couples in the South where today they are being ostracized because of who they are, with North Carolina and other states legislating against the freedom of folks. To be in a room with that group of folks . . . you are like, 'OK, all the hard work we put in there comes together in a moment, in an energy.'"

And as Afropunk spreads its wings and travels to new countries, the DNA of what they stand for has found new fans in other communities around the world. "We had 6,000 people in Paris; we'll have 10,000 in London," Jocelyn says. "It's so needed, people are so excited. Because of the African diaspora and the Caribbean diaspora there, France is really changing and people don't know how to handle it. There's nothing like Afropunk in Europe at all; the people really rally around. . . . You got folks that are coming from Germany and Amsterdam and . . . everywhere that come to Afropunk Paris shows. It's beautiful."

Why We Love This Example: In an era where race and gender are ever more politicized, Afropunk provides a safe space for all those millennial and Gen Z kids who don't quite fit in anywhere else to freely express themselves. Against the backdrop of #BlackLivesMatter and battles for bathrooms breaking out in the South, having a place like the Afropunk Festival, where transgender kids of color can walk around hand in hand with the ones they love, is hugely important. As America approaches becoming a majority-minority country by 2050, Afropunk is the shape of the future: vibrant, confident, inclusive, and supercool.

Chapter 7

Don't Advertise, Solve Problems

Marketers have access to so many tools in our toolbox, but all too often we rely on the same ones over and over again (banner ads, coupons, direct mail) without questioning their efficacy. What if we started using all the tools in our toolbox to come up with something different?

In this chapter we look at new models of creating content and experiences that are either useful or delightful and that help solve problems from "the everyday to the epic."

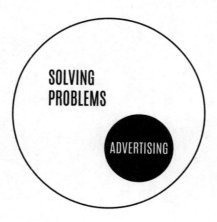

We learn from former Citibank CMO Elyssa Gray about how their investment in the Citi Bike program in New York has led to significant returns for the brand—and created a new public transport system that is now part of the city. Peter Koechley, cofounder of the media company Upworthy, shares how they're creating a new model of positive content that brands can align themselves with. And we meet Marco Vega from the small agency We Believers, which created edible six-pack rings that can help save marine life—an idea that has taken the beer industry by storm.

Elyssa Gray,
Head of Creative and Media, Citibank

We live in a time when we are bombarded by commercial messages—some estimates say more than 5,000 a day. Our cities have turned into cluttered spaces where brands jostle for position on every available space. What if there was a wiser, more useful way to spend all those dollars? Elyssa Gray was the Head of Creative and Media at Citibank when they embarked on a journey that would change the face of New York City.

Of all the case studies we have explored, the Citi Bike story may be the one that best embodies how a marketing investment in a community (instead of in advertising) can reap amazing rewards for a brand.

The story begins with the financial crash of 2008: Citibank took an estimated $476 billion in taxpayer bailouts, more than any other bank. Its brand was in the doghouse, along with many of the other banks involved in the meltdown. Fast-forward to 2012, and Citibank gets a call from NYC mayor Mike Bloomberg's office, asking if they would be interested in underwriting the bike program. After some haggling, Citibank came on board to the tune of $41 million over a six-year period (MasterCard also came on subsequently to underwrite the payment system for around $6.5 million).

For those unfamiliar with the program, the concept is simple. Members pay an annual fee of $149, which enables them to rent bikes from stations positioned strategically around Manhattan (and some parts of Brooklyn) for an unlimited amount of rides per year—the only limitation being that each ride lasts no longer than 45 minutes. Alternatively, for those looking for a shorter-term commitment, there are also 24-hour and seven-day passes as well.

Elyssa Gray, who was Citibank's head of creative and media at the time, was one of a small group of people involved in the project from its inception. She took some time to talk to us about how it all started. She says, "It was definitely hard. It was a bit of an unknown. It was a small group of people who developed the business case for why we thought this was worth taking that leap. There definitely were a lot of concerns around safety, for instance; but we really did our due diligence with the city, with other bike-share programs, and it turns out that accidents go down with bike-share programs.

"Once we demonstrated the value of it, because it was a large investment and it was a multiyear deal, which we don't tend to do . . . people got comfortable. It wasn't easy to sell it, but people definitely saw the value."

She explains how this small team of people managed to stay passionate as they developed the program: "Our brand was at a place where, in our hometown of New York, we wanted to make sure we were doing something unique and disruptive. This program presented itself, and at first we had the same reaction, the same fears . . . but as we dug in and really thought about what this could do, we got excited and started to feed off each other. Once we were all excited about it, and developed that business case to sell it in, that was the first step."

An important part for the New York–based team was putting themselves into the mindset of their fellow New Yorkers—and dealing with some of the setbacks along the way. Elyssa explains, "As a marketer, for me personally, and for my team, when we thought about what we were doing, the positive impact it could have on the city that we lived in, we became personally involved. We did everything: we designed the logo, the name, the bikes, how we would launch this. . . . If you remember, we had *Hurricane Sandy* in the midst of all of this, so we got delayed; many bikes were ruined in the hurricane because they were stored in the Brooklyn Navy Yard. There was plenty of opportunity for us to be stopped, but we took it on the chin because we felt it was the right thing to do. People got passionate about it; people started raising their hands to work on the project, so that was exciting. We always say, 'We are not saving lives, but we are impacting people in a very positive way.'"

Elyssa describes the impact of the program, saying, "Awareness of Citi's association is now probably one hundred percent. It's the largest and most well-known bike share in the country." As of 2023, Citi Bike had reached the staggering figure of more than 100 million rides. There are 180,000 annual subscribers, and monthly average ridership numbers increased above 100,000 for the first time in June 2021. The all-time record for ridership in a single month occurred in August 2023, when the system had 4.07 million rides (Citi Bike, 2024a).

From an environmental point of view, since the system's launch, Citi Bike riders have pedaled more than 120 million miles and offset more than 97 million pounds of carbon and counting. By all measures its been a phenomenal success (Citi Bike, 2024b).

But aside from the raw impressions, perhaps the most impressive return on investment has come in the shift in perception of Citibank. Elyssa explains, "After ten months, we saw rises of sixteen percent of people having a more favorable impression of Citi, eighteen percent rises in the likelihood of considering a Citi product, fifteen percent increases in Citi being an innovative company, and thirteen percent increases of Citi 'enabling progress.' To crown it all, there was a twelve percent increase in those who thought that 'Citi is a socially responsible company.'"

Elyssa tells us what surprised her most about the reaction to the program. "When it launched, I was truly amazed and eternally satisfied that New Yorkers totally embraced this. The creativity that people have had with Citi Bike, whether it's their Tumblr pages, people getting their wedding photos on the bike . . . I think how it's part of New York City now, which is so phenomenal. I think there was even something in *Vogue* or [on *Today*] about how our blue was the 'it' color for spring! The way it just totally got into pop culture so quickly has been really fun. The response from New York has been so amazing."

Celebrities such as Leonardo DiCaprio have been spotted on the bikes, and Bruce Willis rode one onto the set of *The Late Show with David Letterman*. The program has connected culturally cool neighborhoods in Manhattan and Brooklyn in new and accessible ways, opening up the fabric of the city and allowing for new cultural exchanges. In fact, in addition to the branding on the bikes and bike stations around New York, and the millions of social media impressions, probably one of the biggest upsides is that "Citi Bike" has now entered the popular vernacular.

Many of the strongest critics of the big banks comprise exactly the kind of demographic that uses Citi Bike—young, urban, socially conscious people, for whom the financial crisis spelled disaster for careers and jobs. Citibank could have used that $41 million on advertising to try and shift public opinion; instead, the Citi Bike program seems to have shifted it far more effectively and meaningfully than anything from an advertising agency.

Elyssa reveals that the program also had a profound impact on employee pride. She says, "I'm a firm believer that our marketing efforts should make people really proud of what we do, and this does give them company pride; so many people have come to me, and they want to get involved. Driving employee engagement is critical, and this is a great opportunity for our employees to feel what we do in a very unique way. We had our one-year anniversary, we gave out annual passes, and it's a real feel-good for those who work in New York (and we launched a bike share in Miami)—so they can see what Citi is doing for those cities."

The brand-building program has also had some positive effects on Citi's business as well. "We offer our customers a fifteen-dollar statement credit for use toward the program when they use their Citi card to buy their annual membership, and we had some great redemption. So even though brand-building and perception was the primary goal, we are seeing directional lifts from a business perspective." In fact, at launch roughly 30% of the Citi Bike annual memberships have been purchased with a Citi debit or credit card.

Elyssa talks about how this program was different from what Citi had done traditionally, saying, "I look at all of the marketing tools that are available to me, within my tool belt, and each one can do different things—some [that] drive awareness or bring you information, and others [that] bring you an emotional connection, which has a great impact, in a real, authentic way. The culture now is so much more about giving back, and people expect that from the companies they do business with."

Chapter 7: Don't Advertise, Solve Problems   169

She goes on to say, "What was so unique about this program was not just that it allowed greater coverage from an advertising and marketing perspective, but it linked so directly to what the Citi brand has stood for over 200 years, which is 'enabling progress.' And that it added such amazing utility into people's lives. That's the secret sauce . . . that's when the magic happens. This is bringing a new form of transportation to the largest city in America. We're really proud of being part of this movement and bringing this program to New York.

"I think about the type of engagement we're having; we're connecting with people on such a human and emotional level. We have made people's life better, and when you can make an impact on a person's life in that way, as a brand, as a company, that's much more powerful than just seeing a billboard on the side of the road. There are times when we have to 'tell,' but we'd rather 'show'—and this is a great way to do that."

Elyssa has since left corporate life to become a professional coach, but it's clear that she has great pride in what her team was able to accomplish with the Citi Bike program. Her parting thought? "I think all of these brands you are exploring in the book are all about putting the customer first; we're not thinking about ourselves. Yes, we have to link and label back to the brand promise, but we approached this as New Yorkers who would participate in the bike-share program: What would we want?"

Why We Love This Example: Citibank could have spent its $41 million on "perishable" advertising and media. But by thinking of citizens, not consumers and empathizing with their needs, they made a huge, tangible difference to the community they were part of. In a world where public infrastructure is crumbling, such public-private models could pave the way for new brands to engage communities in new and meaningful ways.

Peter Koechley

Cofounder, Upworthy

The oversaturation of commercial messaging doesn't get any better when you look at content on the Web. Here's a startling fact: every second one hour of content gets uploaded to YouTube. That's a decade's worth of content a day. More than any human being could ever consume in a lifetime. In today's frantic media universe, there is a lot of sound and fury but sometimes little meaning. One of the standouts in this new media world is Upworthy, which has built an enormous following around creating meaningful, nourishing video content— that just happens to get massive, viral-worthy engagement around the world.

They've been called "BuzzFeed with a soul"; they are the masters of writing stories with irresistible headlines to draw you in—but then also give you stories so inspiring that you can't help but share them. Perhaps that is part of the secret of their success; they currently have more than 14 million monthly unique users, generating more than 250 million video views per month.

We met with the affable Peter Koechley, one of the cofounders of Upworthy, to talk about their philosophy and how they got started as a media company with a mission. He's now the head of marketing at Rewire America, the leading electrification nonprofit helping people electrify their homes.

Koechley says, "I think it's rare for media to be actually mission-driven. A lot of people are in media for the right reasons, but when you look at media companies, most of them are not driven with an underlying purpose. For us, purpose came even before the form of a media company. My cofounder and I were sitting around in 2011, before we launched, and we just had this feeling that the whole media ecosystem was changing. And it was going from newspapers to newsfeeds; it was my cofounder, Eli Pariser, who first had the realization that actually the stories that matter in the world are just going to disappear if the only way you see them is if your friends want to share them.

"The reason that's true is that it's not because people don't care about these stories, but it's because those stories have never had to be great stories. When you can put something on the front page of a newspaper, when you can dictate that it's at the top of the newscast, you can put your finger on the scale and kind of force it on people; and then you actually give people the choice [of] what to pay attention to. They're going to pay attention to great, compelling stories first, and important stuff kind of second. People don't seek out important things. They seek out great stories, they seek out great culture, they seek out connections to other human beings, and you

172 GOOD IS THE NEW COOL GUIDE TO MEANINGFUL MARKETING

have to actually embed meaningfulness and importance in those interactions and those stories in order for them to thrive on their own. The stories didn't have to compete before, and now they would.

"And so the only way for society to actually get the nourishment it needs (because I think people have this hunger for meaning and a hunger for purpose), you need to make the stories and issues and the topics actually compelling and great and surprising and delightful and wonderful. And if you do that, people will flock to them."

Upworthy is a great example of how to "lead with the cool, but bake in the good." It is one of the modern-day masters in media about how to wrap a meaningful message in an attractive story and deliver it seamlessly to a hungry audience.

Peter says, "We say a lot that Upworthy is premised on two beliefs about human nature. One is that people are better than they get credit for [being], and the other is that they're worse than they get credit for [being] in any given moment. And so, every person, myself included, we go through a day making a thousand short-term bad decisions that maximize shininess and delight over substance and purpose and meaning, but at the end of the day, I will feel empty, and I will feel hollow, and I'll feel like I'm lacking something deeper and richer, and that feels bad.

"And if you can actually connect people with things immediately, with a sense of something that is interesting to see—it's great, it's compelling, it's fascinating, it's cool, it's hip, whatever, and then you deliver, almost by surprise, 'That was surprisingly nourishing. That actually changed how I think about things. That actually touched me on a deeper level,' you build a bond with them. That's what people really want, even if they don't seek it themselves in any given microsecond."

Peter talks about how his own habits as a media consumer guided the form of what he and his cofounder wanted to create: "It's a thing that I feel really personally, because I'm not a great media consumer. Most of my critiques about myself are about how little I read, and how I wish I was just a voracious consumer of information. I'm actually not. I'm busy with my life, I have kids, I run a company, and I let that get in the way. I kind of wanted to create a media company for people like me. Because I can get lost and sucked down into the inanity and the pettiness of life, the sort of pedestrian day-to-day. And I really crave that feeling of deeper purpose and meaning.

"I get it when I'm with my sons and they're being amazing and tomboyish and great, but at the larger level, I want to be drawn towards the best version of myself, and I'm just as attracted to the shiny objects as everyone else. And I'm also not from a religious tradition. There's not a part of my life or my week that holds me to a commitment. So I felt like there must be a lot of people like me, and if we could create a media company for them that drew on their natural human desire for entertainment and engagement and surprise and delight, but actually channeled that towards the better version of themselves—the one that cares about other people, the one that thinks about big issues, the one that helps somebody else in the world—then it's actually a real service to every person we touch, and it's worth starting a business.

"So we hired a couple of curators who were going to help find the stories from the web, and we gave them the mandate to look for things that if a million people saw them, the world would be a better place. And people interpret it very differently from each other—and we were fine with that. We started with the mission of 'How do we get people to pay attention to really important issues? How do we make them compelling and interesting and enjoyable?' And we realized that a big part of the answer is by adding a bit of hope to the story. So I think we're believers that the combination of purpose and hope makes things dramatically more sharable and gives you the opportunity to touch a lot more people.

"I think the other thing that we get a lot from our audience is, 'Wait, I thought you guys were all positive. This is about prison reform. This is not positive.' And our take there is that we're not all positive. I think the things we try to avoid are disempowering, overcomplicated, forbidding, and sort of hopeless. We did a thing on suicide the other day. Not a positive topic. But it was about the semicolon tattoos that people are getting, and one of our writers saw the tattoos, researched, and figured out and discovered that . . . they're tattoos that people get after they've seriously considered suicide and then decided to continue their life. So they're saying, 'As the author of my life, I'm not ending the sentence; I'm going to continue.'"

Upworthy's willingness to deal with some of the darkest parts of humanity in a positive manner is a great counterpoint to those who call the content provider "smarmy" or "smug." Peter says, "It's beautiful! And it's an example of hopeful and inspiring, but looking straight at the existential darkness of suicide, which is a major problem in our society today. So I think we do as much of that. We're not Pollyannaish about the world. We just think that if somebody reads one of our stories and leaves it kind of leaning back or slumping back in their chair and wanting to get back into the bed they just got out of, we haven't done any good in the world. We want active emotions. We want to make people feel activated. The word we use for positivity is 'elevating.' Sometimes it's inspired and lifted up. Sometimes it's like an elevated heart rate. We want to get your heart going."

Part of the success of Upworthy has been its very quick and adept mastering of one of the most powerful forms of storytelling for this audience: mobile video. Peter tells us, "Videos are a huge part of what we're doing, and they're growing every day as a percentage of what we do. The stories on the site are basically all original in one form or another. The videos are licensed videos from tons of partners, and then we make our own as well. It's probably three-quarters licensed and one-quarter originals, something like that, but it's something that will shift over time. Licensing the other videos is something that we believe in. It's a part of being a mission-driven organization. As a media company, we should make all of our original videos, and we can monetize them better . . . there's all sorts of business reasons for it. [But] as a mission-driven company, if I'm an Upworthy fan and I get a video that some individual made that's great, or one of our media competitors made, or it was from some TV show, I'm happy as a fan. If it makes me care about something or feel something, it doesn't really matter. It's only in the interests of the company that makes us want to do more. . . . We're actually doing more and more original stuff because we feel that we can actually tell some stories that other people are missing, that we feel that can be added into the conversation. But every time we see a great story that somebody else had started, then we can just lift that up. We're great with that."

There is great potential for Upworthy to be the "Netflix of good news," finding and curating the best videos from around the world, as well as producing their own original content to create a portfolio of great stories for people to access. "We think a lot about Netflix," Peter says. "Our strategy to date has been, 'Let's really learn about what people like and want. Let's really build data and technology and a huge audience and study what works and what doesn't.' And now we're making our own stuff that is much better than it would be, because it's built on four years of understanding.

"This is really a golden age of media. And I think one of the things that's making it that is we have more access to data and more access to audience feedback than we've ever had before. There was a time in storytelling where you were sitting around a campfire, and you [could] tell when people [were] nodding, when people [were] tearing up, when people [were] standing up and walking away because they [were] bored, or somebody [fell] asleep and [fell] off the log. Then there was this weird couple-hundred-year era of media where you would print something [that got] totally disseminated, and you had no idea [what happened to it]. So people stopped caring whether the audience cared. I mean, live musicians could still tell, stand-up comedians could still tell, but not if you were a newspaper writer or even largely a TV producer, though they still had some data.

"So we view this moment where we can say, 'I have a draft of a story. I can show it to my editor and my editor can give me some notes. I can also show it to a thousand random people on the Internet and see how they react to it' [as] a creative opportunity to see what works and what doesn't. And I trust my own creativity to a certain extent. But I actually trust the aggregate view of a thousand other people a lot. I think if they're all bored and they all don't read more than halfway through, then I can think it's great, but I'm probably wrong. And so we view the interplay between real-time data and audience feedback, and human creativity and ingenuity and intuition; both of them are incredibly valuable. And the real art is breaking up the process so you use data and technology in the moments when it can be the best solution, and you use human creativity when there's no substitute for that. So it's in the mixture there."

Upworthy has successfully partnered with brands ranging from Unilever (with whom they did a story around global warming) to media network the CW (to talk about early detection of pancreatic cancer).

"We're building our business at the intersection of two huge forces," Peter says. "One is this shift among brands to purposeful messages. They know what it's all about, but they know that if they want to reach millennials (and really all modern consumers) then they have to speak with authenticity and meaning and purpose, or they're just not gonna care. So that's a huge shift for them.

"Then the other is this huge shift from basically all other forms of media to mobile video. Mobile video is incredibly in ascendance, and as TV declines and other things decline, it skyrockets upwards. So brands are having a harder time reaching people on TV. They're facing ad blockers and other things that may interrupt their form of advertising and make program interruption kind of difficult. What we do is we create branded, sponsored content, stories with brands that people organically want to share themselves. It's content that is designed to be actually satisfying, because it's filled with purpose and because it's a great story."

Peter talks about some of the examples of brands Upworthy has worked with that have done it right: "We have this video series called Humanity for the Win. And Dignity Health said, 'We like this series; we want to align with it. Do you have something that's related to the medical field a little bit?' And we said yes. 'Great, we'll take this one off the slate and make it and consult with you guys.' The result was a wonderful story about the e-NABLE community who build prosthetics using 3-D printers for kids around the world.

"So that's a great one. We made a great video for Whirlpool that I really liked. You know, Whirlpool is an appliance company seeking to be a lot more than that. They were focused on, like, 'You don't wash laundry just because you want to wash laundry, you wash laundry because you care about your family; care just means so much. And care comes not through grand gestures but from a million easily ignorable, underappreciated gestures.' So we made a video about this great Haitian family living in Queens, where the pretty cantankerous grandma and the teenage son and the two mums all live in the same house. And it kind of profiles one of the mums and her holding the house together. So it's like only loosely about . . . we never mention Whirlpool, but it shows her taking care of the family. It shows her holding them all together, also dealing with her cranky mum and her sweet son. It's very hard work." The content went on to win many plaudits for its heartwarming tale, part of a campaign that helped Whirlpool sales rise 6.6% in the months after it ran.

There is a tricky balance between a brand using its resources to spark debate about a particular issue without then getting a backlash because it is seen to be exploiting the issue without providing solutions. Peter has a nuanced view about the pros and cons of this approach. He says, "I can argue both sides of it. I think if we're going to spend $100 million a year on advertising and we can get twenty percent of that to be pro-social messages that are about a more diversity-inclusive and progressive world, I'll take it. Even if it's not connected to a great CSR initiative, if it's not connected to a great system."

In addition to brands, Upworthy also does a lot of work with nonprofits, helping them get their messages out in powerful and compelling ways. "So it's about a third of our business or something like that. And we're working with the Gates Foundation, we're working with the Open Society Foundation, we're working with a lot of the biggest and smartest foundations out there. With smaller nonprofits, marketing is expensive and it's just a hard case to make. If you're the Gates Foundation and you're going to put $10 billion into global health and poverty stuff, and you actually want to shift public opinion on it, media's a great investment. If you're a small nonprofit that's either going to spend a dollar adding a bed to your homeless shelter or running a campaign with us, we tell you to add another bed. I think there's a very useful role for actually getting the world to care about issues, so we work with people who have the means and the focus in the right place to do that. One of the great things about nonprofits—and this is true about the smartest brands as well—is they actually care about results. So we've spent a lot of time working specifically with the Gates Foundation but using it with others to develop methodology and approach that's scientifically rigorous to look at the effect of our stories on people, the impact that our stories are having. So we can look at a campaign of stories and see how they affect the people who saw the . . . how they affect the attitudinal shift."

Chapter 7: Don't Advertise, Solve Problems   179

Upworthy is also increasingly working with some architects of cool who, for example, may be filmmakers more versed in telling long-form stories but who need assistance in translating that into the fast-paced, short-attention-span world of digital video. "A lot of the people coming to us are filmmakers," Peter says. "Kathryn Bigelow, who directed *Zero Dark Thirty*, came to us and said, 'Hey, I care about the elephants and the ivory trade. I made this amazing PSA. Can we work together?' And we [said], 'Let's do it!' Sheryl Sandberg came to us when she was doing the follow-up campaign to *Lean In*, and now we're doing more work with Facebook because they do more social marketing. People come to us. Largely filmmakers . . . come to us and say, 'I care about this issue. I get how to tell a great story; help me connect it to the world of digital mobile social distribution for that. I can tell a ninety-minute story; help me find the three-minute story in here.' I think that's the cultural community; those are our most frequent partners. We're interested in collaborating in all sorts of ways. In the past we've worked with Shepard Fairey, with his poster in the 2008 [presidential] campaign and things like that."

As Upworthy looks to the future, we discuss the potential of new storytelling platforms such as virtual reality to help continue the great work they are doing. Peter says, "We think that a huge part of our role in the world is spreading empathy, and I think media historically has been kind of civic-minded media, which has been focused a lot on getting the facts out to people and rooting out corruption at the highest levels, both of which are very important roles. I think the third role, though, is this role of empathy. Democracy is a crazy idea—the idea that I'm going to accept some compromise in my life . . . you know, that I'll pay a tax so that somebody that I've never seen and don't understand and don't care about has a better life. Like so many of the big, amazing ideas in our world, that's really counterintuitive. And it only works if you actually care about everyone. And so the fact that we can get ten million people around the world to watch the same video that makes a group think . . . like, *Oh, I get them. They're humans, they're just like me,* that's really powerful. So we focus on that with mobile social video. I think VR is a great extension of that, and I'm excited to see it develop."

After our conversation, we saw a powerful example of Upworthy's mission in action. Speaking on a Reddit AMA, Peter addressed the Brussels attacks, which happened earlier that day:

"I think moments of tragedy are often the most important times to spread hope. Because they're some of the hardest times to find it. Days like today are hard. The world is full of really terrible things. Not just terrorism, but discrimination, injustice, institutional racism, grinding poverty. At Upworthy, we look for hopeful stories of people making change, because to make the world work, we actually all need to do that. And if you're feeling totally defeated, you're not going to stand up and start doing something to fix a problem in your life or your town or the world.

"So when something horrific like Brussels happens, we look for how people pull together in the response. Like people in Brussels using the hashtags #IkWillHelpen ('I want to help') and #PorteOuverte ('open house') to offer shelter to those with nowhere to stay. We don't want to amplify the hatred and vitriol, we want to draw attention to the folks standing up against it."

We couldn't have said it better ourselves.

Why We Love This Example: Upworthy is an example of a mission-driven media company that is challenging the norms of what "news" is and should be. Their purpose is to bring a daily dose of meaning into everyone's lives, and their results speak to the powerful desire they have uncovered within their audience for stories of purpose and optimism. We feel if more news organizations shifted away from their diet of carnage and outrage, it could create a groundswell of public opinion and activism that could help do a lot more good in the world.

Marco Vega

Cofounder, We Believers

Along with great storytelling, one of the most useful tools brands can use is the power of design. Great marketing can also be about refining the product experience to make it more useful or delightful to the end user. In this example, we look at how a tiny agency made headlines around the world when it took the humble plastic six-pack rings and transformed them into something that made a profound difference to the environment.

We meet Marco Vega at the Cannes Lions International Festival of Creativity, the biggest advertising festival in the world, in the beautiful city of Cannes, France. For this week, the city is awash in brands taking over the beach huts and yachts to hawk their wares and preach the gospel of advertising, while promotional teams hand out mini samples of everything from bottled water to bottled oxygen (we're not kidding).

It is perhaps an ironic place to talk about how brands should stop advertising and solve problems instead, but it is also a place where this theme seems to be strongly resonant in the work that is winning. Outdoor clothing brand REI's Opt Outside campaign, which closed down their stores on the biggest shopping day of the year, Black Friday, and encouraged consumers to stop shopping and go into nature, has just won a Grand Prix, the highest award you can win. And Keith Weed, the idiosyncratic CMO of Unilever, makes a presentation about how the major multinationals' five top-growing brands all have either sustainability or social conscience at their heart. Change is in the air.

Marco is exultant, having won multiple Cannes Lion awards (two golds, one silver, and one bronze) for the work that his small agency, We Believers, has done in creating the world's first edible six-pack rings for beer companies, beating out massive brands like Google, Netflix, and Audi. He speaks with the passionate intensity of someone who has found his true calling. The agency he and his partner, Gustavo Lauria, started began with the conviction that there had to be a better way forward in marketing. On their website, they make their philosophy explicit: "The best way to solve a business problem is to focus on solving people's problems and fulfilling people's needs."

The problem We Believers set out to fix was plastic waste in the world's oceans, one of the most significant environmental problems today. Research from Greenpeace shows that 80% of sea turtles and 70% of seabirds are ingesting plastic today, not to mention the massive floating landfills of trash that infest the sea, caused by more than

12 billion tons of plastic entering the world's oceans every year. And plastic six-pack rings for beer are one of the biggest culprits, well-known for entangling and strangling fish, birds, and other wildlife.

The solution We Believers came up with for their client, Saltwater Brewing—a small beer company based in Florida—was deceptively simple. Why not use the waste material used in the production of beer—the wheat, the barley—to create biodegradable and edible six-pack rings that could be harmlessly ingested by the wildlife instead of strangling them? The conservation-conscious client, who regularly worked with marine conservation charities, immediately saw the potential in the design.

Marco believes this can be the zero waste, zero carbon footprint for the entire industry. And the PR and buzz around the announcement have been huge, with hundreds of millions of positive impressions for the project in PR and social media. And in Cannes he shared with us that in the scant six weeks since the project was announced, more than 250 brewers had already contacted them to express an interest in signing up—including some of the biggest names in the business such as AB InBev, Heineken, and Miller-Coors. That was truly indicative that this had moved from being an idea to the start of a bigger movement.

When asked what makes We Believers' philosophy different, Marco's answer shows the conviction of his beliefs. He says, "We Believers is a place with a start-up attitude. When you truly believe and create, good things and people follow. We Believers is a place that believes in people, a place defined by its ideas and not technology as a substitute for ideas. We believe in conversations above the presentations, in 'trust us from the beginning.'" As Marco's partner Gustavo states elegantly: "For brands to be successful today, it is no longer about being the best in the world—but rather, being the best *for* the world and taking a real stance."

WE ARE FACING

AN ERA WHERE

HUMANITY WILL SHED

THOSE BRANDS WHOSE

PRODUCTS DO NOT

SOLVE A NEED.

—MARCO VEGA

And when questioned about the potential for brands to "stop advertising and start solving problems," Marco's answer is equally unequivocal: "We are facing an era where humanity will shed those brands whose products do not solve a need, fail to commit to fix a cause, and fall short to fuel movements to bring people together. I believe wholeheartedly this is the way to go for business under a Conscious Capitalism umbrella. The advertising industry, however, is proving to be deadly slow to catch up."

Marco believes that the answer to getting agencies to catch up to what consumers and brands want is to come up with a completely new paradigm and mindset. He says, "Stop thinking like an agency. Start thinking like a venture capitalist or angel investor for good ideas. You are going to spend the next couple of months solving for that problem. You will invest a chunk of hours [in] it, so it might as well be something you truly believe in together with your client. The days of the SOW (Statement of Work) with a list of deliverables might not be gone, but you don't want to be caught in one of them. Focus on work that matters, shed work that 'needs to get done.'"

When asked about what other brands and work he thinks act in the same vein, Marco is honest enough to admit that inspiration isn't easy to find. "This is probably the question I battled the most to answer," he says. "When it [comes] to solving problems in people's lives, there are none. At least none I can think of that are not associated with an NGO or not-for-profit. We all talk about TOMS, Patagonia, Ben & Jerry's as flagships of Conscious Capitalism. However, none of them were to be found as festival winners. Even worse, Blake Mycoskie, TOMS founder, received an honorary award. Yet there was no TOMS work awarded in any category. So there's still a sense of [disingenuousness] going on at the festival. That is why the work we did for Saltwater Brewing makes me so proud. It's a creative idea which resulted in an invention that 'builds the brand' and 'starts a movement.' The invention is for ocean conservancy.

The brand is about ocean conservancy. An authentic approach to brand building."

Marco's final advice for those in agency land who are seeking a similar path toward meaningfulness? "Do stuff that you are truly passionate about. If there is no passion, there is no drive to tear down the walls that will come towards you to squash your project. If you don't have that passion, you will get squashed. If you do have the passion, that wall, once you clear it, will make your idea better."

Why We Love This Example: With Americans drinking more than 6 billion gallons of beer a year, the potential to scale this idea and make it even more cost-effective is huge. Not to mention the potential reapplicability across other industries that have similar packaging issues that cause environmental waste. It is a phenomenal example of how brands can practice "cradle-to-cradle" design principles in an enlightened way across the full life cycle of what they produce. And how the creativity inherent in the advertising industry can pivot toward solving problems through design, not just stories.

Chapter 8

People Are the New Media

In today's world, the Holy Grail of marketing is positive word of mouth. And thanks to the digital revolution, people can become your biggest advocates—at a scale that can rival even traditional paid media.

In this section, we hear the inspiring story of Kfir Gavrieli and Tieks, who unleashed the power of kindness in their community to sew face masks for frontline workers. Jaha Johnson, the manager of artists such as Common and Usher, discusses how they use their work and fan base to drive social consciousness around issues such as Black Lives Matter. And Josie Naughton, from the inspiring non-profit Choose Love, shares how they use the power of their community to raise hundreds of millions of dollars to help refugees and displaced people around the world.

Kfir Gavrieli

Cofounder
Tieks

Fashion brand Tieks has provided a remarkable example of how a brand can mobilize its community to do good. After learning of the shortage of face masks, the brand challenged its community to #SewTOGETHER, a campaign that has lit up social media and helped generate 1 million masks for frontline medical workers (in return for which Tieks gave them gift cards). It's a remarkable example of how even small brands can create a lot of good by enlisting the help of their customers.

Tieks is a fashion brand beloved by women who are fans of their comfortable, durable ballet flats. The Tieks community (which reportedly includes Oprah, who included them on her O-List) is passionate about their experiences with the shoes, posting on Facebook about how they wear them at momentous occasions such as graduations or funerals. So it was no surprise that when the pandemic hit and the brand reached out to them to help frontline workers, the response was immediate and massive. We caught up with CEO and cofounder Kfir Gavrieli to learn more about his company's journey, how this noble initiative came about and what other brands can learn from their experience.

He shared the company's humble beginnings. "We launched Tieks with little prior experience in fashion in 2008. We spent the first two years perfecting the Tieks shoe design. I wanted something that would be simultaneously comfortable, durable, fashionable, and portable—a combination of features that didn't exist in an industry that dates back millennia. We are deeply invested in providing a best-in-class product, while making a positive impact on the world."

Social impact has been embedded into the company from inception—manifesting in a partnership with micro-loan organization Kiva. "Our mission as a company is to empower women, and one way we do that is through a shoe designed to be uniquely versatile. Another way we advance that mission is by making loans through the Kiva platform to women entrepreneurs living in poverty. I went to business school with Jessica Jackley, the cofounder of Kiva, and knew immediately that Kiva's mission dovetailed with our ethos at Tieks," said Kfir.

Through loans ranging in size from $25 to over $1000, Kiva allowed Tieks to provide much needed working capital to women entrepreneurs in places where there is no easy access to small loans. This made a huge difference in women's ability to start businesses, provide for their families, and in many cases, transform their communities. Through the Gavrieli Foundation, Tieks has become the largest single lender on Kiva, contributing more than $10 million to thousands of women entrepreneurs in 70 countries, including the United States.

Kfir shared how the inspiring facemask initiative came about. "In March, a friend whose sister is a doctor told me that her hospital would be out of masks within a couple of weeks. I was shocked—and scrambled to figure out how I could help get personal protective equipment (PPE) into the hands of our frontline medical providers. I partnered with some other entrepreneurs to try and purchase medical masks overseas, but the procurement proved very challenging. At the same time, we retooled our Los Angeles facility and retrained our staff to sew masks that we could donate. Quickly, we realized that we were sitting on a much bigger resource: our millions of customers and fans."

Tieks launched Operation #SewTOGETHER to solicit mask donations from our customers for frontline heroes. Their website provides detailed instructions on how to make masks at home and offered up to $100 Tieks gift cards for 50 masks donated. Overnight, they saw thousands of dedicated volunteer sewers take up this cause across the country, producing more than 1 million masks in living rooms, around kitchen tables, and converted basements.

Kfir is moved when he shared the response. "We received masks from teachers who are working from home, sewing masks on their lunch break and when they're off the clock. We saw neighborhoods form sewing groups to encourage each other to join in the effort. We've received emotional emails from laid-off workers looking to do their part to fight the virus. Our social media channels are a continuous source of motivation, as thousands of medical providers have reached out to share just how much this effort means to them. It was humbling to be part of this nationwide, lifesaving effort."

In closing, Kfir shared, "Obviously, the novel coronavirus is viral in a way that has been catastrophic for our world. The way you contend with something that's viral in a bad way, is to create something that's viral in a good way. Through #SewTOGETHER, we combated the spread of coronavirus by highlighting how the best of humanity—generosity and caring about others—can spread virally in a good way. People want to help. When you empower them to be part of a solution, it is contagious."

Why We Love This Example: By creating a simple act that so many of their community could participate in, Tieks helped give agency and meaning to so many people who were powerless—and found a way to tap into the incredible power of kindness and the desire to contribute to the common good. We hope more brands are inspired to create platforms like #Sewtogether in a way that helps unlock the superpowers of their communities and make them active participants in doing good.

Jaha Johnson

Manager, Common and Usher

Jaha Johnson believes in this age when fans are demanding more transparency and access, authenticity is more essential than ever from the artists themselves and the art they create. Jaha shares how that expectation is inspiring artists such as Usher and Common to be more open about the social issues they care about and to create music that reflects their passions and moves people to action . . . and how a near-death experience has helped him embrace his own purpose for helping others.

Jaha Johnson has worn many hats in his career: manager and creative collaborator for some of the biggest artists in the world, including Mary J. Blige, Common, and Usher; music label executive; mentor; confidante; and cultural tastemaker. He is now the founder of an R&B record label called November Yellow. When a freak surfing accident left him helplessly paralyzed from the neck down, lying alone on the shore of the beach, sinking deeper and deeper into the wet sand, watching as each wave of water that washed over his face seemingly brought him closer to death, none of those titles mattered. He was simply a father praying to see his son again, and a man hoping to continue a life that suddenly felt incomplete.

Jaha miraculously survived that day, and has since recovered to full health with a renewed sense of purpose and urgency that he applies to his life and work. As we sit down to talk with Jaha in his Brooklyn home, he is wrapping up a call on a potential deal for his client, hip-hop artist, actor, and activist Common. He speaks with a noticeable combination of confidence and curiosity. He has a boldness and brashness that have helped make him a respected voice in his field, but he's equally inquisitive—intrigued and inspired by the possibilities that have yet to be explored.

Jaha tells the story of the day he realized his "why," how that realization has inspired him to help use the unique power of music to engage fans in social change, what a near-death experience taught him about himself, and how much more he still has to give. As a student at Clark University, Jaha started his career interning at different record labels, and he had a pivotal turning point one day as an intern at LaFace when he was an interning for Shanti Das (the promotions person there).

Jaha says, "At the same time I was at LaFace, I also interned for a regional rep from RCA Records, and my job then was to call radio stations and get them to play the records, and I remember just hearing a bunch of records that I didn't like, and everything at LaFace for the most part I liked. So I remember I didn't really know the co-founders but I was bold and inquisitive and stopped one of them in the hallway. I said 'What do you do if you don't like what you're being told to sell?' And he said, 'The two most important roles at a record label are the man who makes the music, which is the A&R, and the man who sells the music, which is the promotion man; everything else in between is administrative. Those are people that are just to get the job done, but someone's got to make the art and someone's got to sell the art.' So he said, 'If you don't like what you're being told to sell, you need to go on the side of making it.'

"And that one conversation changed everything for me. I was like, 'OK, so what does that mean?' So then I started researching and getting into producing. I started managing producers, and that's when I got down with Noontime [Records] and I started getting into the art of making the records. And it was like a drug for me. I've never felt such a rush because I'm involved in making this. And this is going to be on the radio, someone's going to like this; this record is going to change someone's life. Because for me, you know, music has always been about the impact it has on each individual.

"I remember the first time I heard that Donny Hathaway 'A Song for You' on a rooftop in Brooklyn with my friend, and her mom had a Donny Hathaway collection, and she played 'A Song for You' and I was psyched. I couldn't even . . . I was stuck; [I'd] never heard a song like that in my life. So for me, that's a feeling I've always wanted to be a part of; I always wanted to make things that stuck with someone's soul, to their ribs, that made them feel something that made them motivated to do something different. So that was that day; that was that moment when I found my purpose: be a part of making the art and finding out where your skill set fits in there."

One of the core values Jaha embraced early on was the importance of authenticity. It has been an essential quality that he looks

Chapter 8: People Are the New Media   197

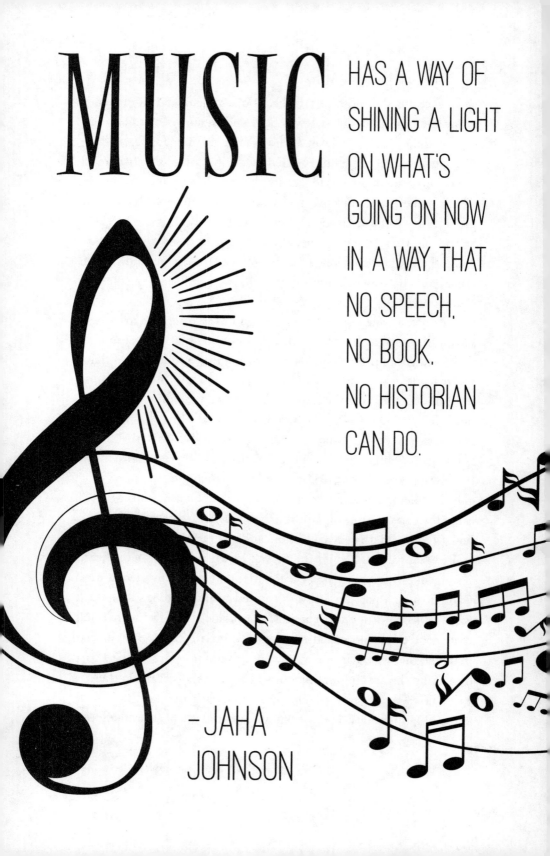

for in his clients and the art they create. He believes in this age when fans are the new media, they are demanding more transparency and access; authenticity is more essential than ever.

"We're in this space now that everything is about authenticity," he says. "Everybody wants to be the truest version of themselves, now more than ever before, and I think that's because on reality TV, things are more fake than they've ever been before. Everybody wants to be more real; it's like you want to be the most honest version of yourself in the most dishonest world. We couldn't be living in a more dishonest time in terms of integrity or who we are as individuals. People are really trying to clamber on to things that they really connect with.

"You know, we laugh and joke about people like DJ Khaled [the respected hip-hop DJ who became a social media sensation from his inspiring messages], but I'm so happy for him. I mean, first of all he is a great person just as a human being, but I'm happy for him because he is inspiring and motivating people. He is doing it and he is not afraid to talk about it and to let people see it. So in this time when reality TV is taking over with so many things that aren't real, when you see people living their true authentic self, that's the reality TV we are supposed to be living in. That's what we are supposed to be watching every day. Whether you like it or not, watching this guy who works so hard and is so passionate about everything he does and is working right now, those are the things you're supposed to follow, because that's real. [There is] nothing fake about what Khalid is doing.

"People want to know what's real about these artists. You want to know what they really mean, what they really stand for: 'What do you care about outside of what you sing in your songs? Is that all you are or are you more?' So I think because there are no more secrets and because there are no more walls, the fans want to know everything about you—what inspires and influences and motivates you. If they don't feel like they know you, they are not into you. And because there are no longer these walls that exist anymore, your audience knows when you're lying.

"I think that made me very conscious of the choices that I make, who I choose to work with, what type of artists . . . I want to sign, that I want to be affiliated with, because, I want to be associated with the real, not keeping it real, but with the 'real,' like that's who you are. I want to make the best version of who you are, not the best version of who you think you are."

When we speak about the seemingly recent shift of artists being more socially active, Jaha believes it's not anything new, but he does see a shift in fans' interest in the issues artists care about. He says, "There are a lot of artists who been doing that kind of work for a long time when there was no social media and there wasn't cool technology the way it is now. Now it's applauded, you get put on a pedestal for doing it. Where before, it was like people didn't care enough or it wasn't cool enough to do those things."

He believes it's a natural evolution for artists to become more socially conscious as they become older and more successful. He tells us, "I think it's a natural trend for all artists, and I credit it to age and access. As you get older as an artist, you have the benefit of being able to travel and see the world from a different view. If you have any type of soul and consciousness, you can't help but be affected by the impact of the things you see, because your box has now grown. So if you're Common from Chicago, while you may have always had some version of consciousness, it's so much different now. You don't just see when it happens in your neighborhood; you now have the benefit of traveling the world, and then it actually makes what's happening at home more important.

"When you first started as a young kid, that's not what you're thinking about. You wanted to be a star. And as you achieve success, you then have the luxury to sit back and pay attention to the things you didn't pay attention to before. Also, when you become a parent, you start to think about the world [your] kids are going to grow up in. You know, as Common sent his daughter off to Howard University last year, as Usher has, you know, a seven-year-old child and an eight-year-old child, it's like you can't help but be aware and pay attention to the world that you are bringing someone into and wonder how you can make it better."

Jaha believes music artists, in particular, have a unique influence in the lives of people, particularly youth. He says, "No one wants to hear their parents telling them what they shouldn't do. But they would rather hear it from somebody they look up to, their favorite sports star or their favorite singer. That's not a small responsibility, you know. When a pastor gets up in church on Sunday, those people are hanging on his words. His interpretation of a book tells people how to get through the week before they come back the next Sunday. That's what artists do! When they speak, the fans are hanging on their words for guidance, for information that says this is how we do it, this is what we should wear, or this where we should go. I can't imagine what that must feel like. It has to be scary to be the person that stands onstage with a thousand eyeballs on you."

Jaha believes as a manager he plays an important role in helping and challenging his artists to execute their artistic visions and make the impact with fans they desire to. He spoke specifically about his relationship with Common and their partnership together, saying, "The most valuable part of our relationship is our conversation. You know, it's like we talked about a song the other day. I told him what was a favorite song for me on his new album, and he called to tell me today, 'I played that song for Michelle and Barack [Obama] on Saturday, and they loved it.'

"He wasn't thinking about that song like that before, and he made it! Because sometimes you need somebody with an objective eye and ear to tell you, you know, 'You did something great! Nah, nah, you're taking it for granted. No, that's a great song! That's not just a song, it's a *great* song. You should be proud of that song! Don't dismiss it.'"

Jaha speaks about their work together on Common's album, *Nobody's Smiling*, inspired by Common's concern about the violence in his hometown, Chicago. That album led to the powerful Oscar-winning song "Glory," which continues to have an impact on the artist and in the ongoing fight for social justice and the end of senseless violence.

"Common is someone who always kind of spoke about these issues," Jaha says. "So he makes this album and, you know, hardcore Common fans and hip-hop fans love the album. But what's great about it was it was the beginning of a cycle that led us to the song 'Glory,' because in the theme of where he was in his life, it's like 'Glory' was the period to the sentence. Because then he goes to do this movie *Selma* about Selma and Martin Luther King Jr. After seeing the movie, he was so moved he called me and said, 'I'm going to make the end title song for this movie.' He wasn't asked to, it wasn't in his deal, and he literally put it together; he called John Legend himself.

"The reason why I said it connects to when we started with the album is, for him, when he saw the movie it reminded him how far we've come and about how far we haven't come. Some of the same things that he is talking about and referencing on his album, he was reminded of when watching *Selma*, so for him, it was like he still has so much work to do.

"And you know, that song—forget winning him an Oscar—it's more about the light that the song was able to shine on him and about what's going on. It's worth more than the Oscar, because once again, it opened up so many conversations, so many dialogues; it help[ed] shine a light [on] the movie, which was important, for young people to see that movie."

That experience reinforces the power music has to reach people in powerful ways. "I always say: 'Music is the soundtrack to everyone's life.' It's a part of every important moment. It's your victory, or it's your funeral song. It's your 'I'm in love' song; it's your 'stand up and do something' song.

"Music has a way of shining a light on what's going on now and what went on then in a way that no speech, no book, no historian can do. Kids have a short attention span, and when you can get to them in three minutes in a song what they get in a class for an hour or for a year course, you can't equate. It's like you can tell me every day to come to school and study this, but this one song inspired me the way that one class is supposed to. That's not to discount or take away from education, or discount or take away from public speakers or reading or anything like that, but songs—music—is the most motivational tool."

We also speak about Usher's active support for the Black Lives Matter movement, and how seeing another young Black male killed by a police officer inspired Usher to create a song that led to one of the biggest music events and fundraisers of 2015. Jaha says, "With Usher specifically, it's a newer space for him to play in publicly. You know, he's had a foundation for years that people weren't aware of, doing a lot of work with Harry Belafonte, the Clintons, and education has always been a big platform for him, but once again these things weren't celebrated the way they are now.

"Last summer, we were in London making the album and another case, something just happened on the news. I can't remember which case it was; it might have been the one in North Carolina where the cop shot the guy in the back. But something happened, and we go to the studio that night and there was this track that the bands were working on, and he starts talking with Bibi, one of the songwriters on his album, about what he wanted to sing. Bibi is from

Berlin and she's young. She's like twenty years old, so a lot of this she doesn't really understand, which in itself was an interesting dynamic to have these two artists writing together, one from a very informed standpoint and the other one from an uninformed standpoint.

"He made the song called 'Change' because he was very passionate about 'This has to stop! You [the police] are here to protect and serve us; you can't keep killing us!' Not all cops are bad, but this is out of hand. It's clearly a pattern with this, and it isn't the first time. And you know I always love when a song is made from a place of passion; it's what's most important to me in my entire career.

"You know, he's so charged up and excited about the song, sending it to a couple of people, and he played it for Jay Z, and Jay called him and said it was the most excited he'd been about a song that he heard in a long time. That song and that conversation ultimately led to the Tidal X concert they had in Barclays. It is because of that song. It was because Jay Z felt his passion, Jay felt moved and decided to come together to raise this money, you know, with the late Harry Belafonte, Black Lives Matter, to really go to support these different initiatives around the country to help change laws, to help families; and how one song can mobilize so many people and such a movement. And for him, that's probably his least successful song; the song wasn't a hit in the sense of radio play and success by the normal standards, but it was a hit and success in terms of what it did.

"You know it led the charge to them raising $1.5 million and it just brought light and awareness, and that song led to him being asked to speak on the American Justice Summit's panel at John Jay College of Criminal Justice and all these different kinds of conversations that opened up. So that one song opened up a light and a pathway to a lot of other conversations that made me proud of him, because that's what you want.

"That's the reason why I do this is to help someone execute their art to bring it to the light to effect change in whichever way. And some change will just be for fun and some change will be to move people."

A year ago, Jaha almost didn't live to see the impact he was helping create in the world. He tells the story of an accident that changed his life. He says, "So the timing of the accident was interesting. A couple of years ago I started . . . well, in 2007 I really started running, by 2009 I got into cycling, and in 2013 I decided that I wanted to do triathlons. I wasn't a great swimmer, but in that same mindset of just wanting to do more and pushing, work[ing] through the personal challenges, it was something that I got into.

"I had started surfing a couple of years ago, because when I got into swimming, I just loved being in the water and I wanted a new challenge, so I got into surfing. So I have a surf instructor, and I would surf with him whenever I could. It wasn't every week, but I just got a new board, a small board, a faster board. So I trained that Sunday morning and then I went out to go for a surfing lesson with my trainer and just kind of went out to get used to the new board. And it wasn't some, like, amazing story where I was on this ten-foot wave. No, I didn't even get up this particular time.

"We've been in the water for a little while, getting used to the board, and a wave was coming and I didn't get up in time, so I was just kind of waiting for the wave to get past me and wait it out. And this particular time, I wasn't even on the board, but the angle of the wave hit me [and] spun me over, and I hit my head on the bottom.

"I wasn't sure what I hit my head on, but I immediately heard this 'pop,' and it was my spine, and I was like, 'Oh, shit!' 'cause I was fully conscious, and it turns me, and then I'm on my back and I'm just like, 'Okay,' but I couldn't get my head out of the water and I couldn't move. Like, I was paralyzed from the neck down. And that's when the reality set in and then everything just kind of went slow motion. I was like, 'Oh, shit! This is really happening. Like I can, like, you know, my eyes are wide open.'

Chapter 8: People Are the New Media   205

"The irony of the eyes-wide-open part is when I was younger and I used to swim, I never loved swimming because the water would always bother my eyes, and every pair of goggles I got would leak, and so I didn't trust the gear. So I was an okay swimmer, but I never swam because I just didn't trust it. And you know, swimming with your eyes closed is pointless underwater, but when I finally got back to swimming a couple of years ago, I trusted my gear; I just went for it and never looked back. And when you surf, you don't have goggles on. You know, I went for it. I'm still not worried about it; water can get in anybody's eyes. But this time, I'm underneath the water and my eyes are wide open, and I could see everything clear as day. So one of my biggest fears before, being water in my eyes—specifically saltwater—it's not even a factor, and I could look up and see my body and I could look up and at first I thought it was the sun, and I believe that it was the sun at first.

"But the light just kept getting brighter and brighter as I started to sink underneath the water, because I couldn't move. And I was trying to stay calm, and I was calm. I wasn't screaming, crying—I wasn't doing anything, but I knew nobody could hear me. So I'm just under the water and I'm just looking at my body drop underneath and then in that last moment, you know, my whole life flashed before me, with reflections on everything—my last conversation with my son Jaden, everything—and then at that last moment my instructor got there and pulled me out."

That profound event has given him a stronger sense of urgency to share more of his gifts with the world. "The accident, for me, it was less about reaffirming my purpose and more about me owning up to my own purpose," he says. "So much of what I do is for everyone else. I had my own version of that in me that I've been pushing to the back, that I haven't been executing on, and a big part of that was fear-based.

"[I asked myself,] 'Why are you not following through on some of the most important pieces of the things that you really want to do, like get your book done? Finish your script. Focus on your life. You're not here to just quietly do your work and sail off into the sunset. You're here to let people know that it's okay to work hard. And that it's okay to dream big and execute and to never stop or that there's no wrong way or there's no one way of doing things, and all these things that I've learned along the way, things that I've tried and failed at or that I can help people not make some of the same mistakes, or it's okay to make some of the same mistakes.'

"When you almost die, you realize how much more living you have to do. It's like death is final on this earth, so if I was to die that day when I said my good-byes and I thought it was over, then whatever I did up to that point, that would've been how my story would have been told. And I'm pretty sure that a lot of people would've been happy with that story, but I wouldn't have been happy with that story. 'Cause I realized that day that there is still so much that I haven't done. There's still so much that I want to teach and that I want to show people; it's not for bragging or stunting, but when you see someone else do it, you have no choice but to feel like you can do it too."

That impact is already being felt on others, starting at home. "I told my son today I went swimming this morning . . . [and] he said, 'That's it?' I said, 'What do you mean by that?' He said, "Well, Dad, you did four workouts yesterday, so today you got to do six workouts.' That's what he said to me. And just for him to think like that, that's all I want. . . . That made me so proud to hear that coming from him to let me know that he is paying attention to what I do and what I say. It didn't go unnoticed. To him it was like, 'Wow, my dad did four workouts yesterday.' So that's what the accident taught me—that I've got a duty to share, to inform, to motivate the same way people did for me. It's like we have to constantly be paying it forward."

Chapter 8: People Are the New Media 207

Why We Love This Example: Too often, as marketers, we find ourselves trying to get others to buy into offerings that we haven't bought into ourselves. We see the offering, and deep down we question its quality or usefulness or authenticity. But yet we try to sell it anyway, and then seem surprised when people don't buy our messages or our products. Jaha's story reminds us, even if we are not creators, we have the opportunity and responsibility to work with those who are—artists, designers, developers—to create things that we can believe in, that move us, that add value to people's lives. That is where the best work happens. It is where the real connections with consumers are made, where their advocacy is born. And even when we feel like we are drowning in a world of inauthenticity, if we open our eyes, we can see clearly there is a better way.

Josie Naughton

Cofounder, Choose Love

Choose Love started back in 2015 when a group of friends began collecting donations for refugees in Calais. They have gone on to become a global organization supporting refugees and displaced people all over the world. We caught up with Josie Naughton, the inspiring CEO and cofounder of Choose Love to find out how they transformed from a small initiative into a global organization helping millions of refugees all over the world.

It's a Wednesday in Rockefeller Center in New York and excited customers are lining up outside a shop like no other. Unlike the glamorous boutiques that surround the area, when people buy things at this store, they walk out with nothing except a warm glow in their hearts. Because here shoppers can buy real items and life-saving interventions which will go to refugees and displaced people across the world. Not every shop can claim that everything it sells will change a life, but for Choose Love, that's the truth.

"Choose Love started seven years ago, as myself and some friends wanting to raise $1000 and collect some aid for refugees during the 'refugee crisis' in 2015. That year over a million people arrived in Europe seeking sanctuary, primarily from Syria but also from Afghanistan, Iraq, Iran, Eritrea, South Sudan to name a few. We were moved, like so many by the image of the little boy Aylan Kurdi who washed up on the Turkish shore and we were driven by a sense of empathy and responsibility for our fellow humans," Josie reflected.

Fast-forward to today and Choose Love is a global organization working in 26 countries to support refugees and displaced people. It does this by partnering with and funding over 200 local community-based organizations, prioritizing organizations led by displaced communities, who are more often than not the primary responders on the front lines of this crisis. It works across the world, including Europe, the Balkans, Ukraine, the Middle East, and the US-Mexico border. Choose Love funds everything from urgent medical care, search and rescue operations, food, humanitarian aid to legal support, and a special focus for support for marginalized communities.

Over the last nine years, through the help of their passionate and engaged global community, they have achieved some incredible things:

- Supported almost 5 million people worldwide.
- With all of their partners, they've distributed more than 5 million hot meals, almost 3 million nappies, and over 650,000 items of clothing.
- They've also rescued over 20,000 people at sea, funded almost 200,000 medical consultations, supported more than 130,000 legal cases, and built almost 60,000 shelters.
- They've funded a total of 393 organizations across the world.

This inspiring nonprofit has also been supported by celebrities such as Benedict Cumberbatch, Harry Styles, Dua Lipa, Jameela Jamil, Olivia Coleman, Trevor Noah, Michael Caine, and many others. They also have received a major multimillion dollar grant from MacKenzie Scott.

The size of refugees and migrants problems globally is massive and it's getting worse. When Choose Love started its work seven years ago, there were 65 million displaced people in the world, and as of 2022, the number is just over 108 million—with approximately half of that number being children. With no resolutions to existing conflicts and the effects of climate change really starting to be felt, this number is continuing to increase. There are estimates that there will be a billion displaced people in the world by 2050. Josie explained, "As the numbers of displaced people increase, so does the need for funding but we are seeing a reduction in global funding for those who are forcibly displaced as well as a political shift to the right, which creates more hostile environments for refugees. Refugees and asylum seekers are having to make heartbreaking choices about whether to buy food or medicine for their children. Given all of this we urgently need to raise more funds to meet the ever increasing needs."

Josie explained how the Choose Love stores worked. "Throughout the store you'll find items and visual representations of services Choose Love provides to refugees and displaced people across the world, spanning winter essentials, life-changing interventions, and long-lasting support. Items available for donation include basic necessities, including winter clothing, hot food, and fuel, as well as much-needed services such as reuniting families, long-term accommodation, evacuation support, and lifesaving medical treatment. Whatever you buy, you don't take away with you; instead we use your donation to buy that product for someone who really needs it this winter. You can even buy one of everything in the whole store for $565." Through the Choose Love stores (both physical and online), their community has bought over 15 million dollars of items to support refugees around the world. It also has a store online www.choose.love for those who can't make it to the physical store.

One hundred percent of funds raised through the shop go to supporting displaced people from all over the world, including working in the Middle East, Greece, on the US-Mexico border, as well as supporting projects in the Ukraine and Gaza. Buying from the Choose Love Shop offers people something that can make a real, tangible difference. "In showcasing basic items in dire need for millions worldwide, we want to not only raise awareness of how displaced people and refugees are stripped of basic necessities but remind those more fortunate of what to be grateful for," Josie shared.

Choose Love recently hit a milestone in helping over 5 million people globally. We talked what it meant to get to this stage. "When we started we never could have imagined that the organization would be working at this scale. In fact we always worked to put ourselves 'out of business' but it's clear the needs are ever increasing and that our work is needed for the foreseeable future," she noted. "We never take the trust people place in us for granted and will always make sure our funds are used as effectively, efficiently, and transparently as possible."

Why We Love This Example: This milestone is incredible because it shows the power of solidarity and what is possible when people come together to make change. Hundreds of thousands of people, from all walks of life and every corner of the globe, have supported Choose Love over the years, and the number of people helped is really testament to every single donor, fundraiser, volunteer, and partner organization that have helped this noble organization make a difference in the world.

Chapter 9

Back Up the Promise with the Proof

Today when every brand is preaching a message of positive empowerment, it is important to back up messaging with action—otherwise, it will be seen either as empty rhetoric or a brand exploiting an issue for commercial gain. We live in an era when consumers not only demand transparency and accountability but also are equipped with tools to call out brands that do not "back up the promise with the proof."

In this section, Laura Probst, former head of social goodness at the Honest Company, reveals how she is "reinventing CSR" to ensure her company makes good on its promise to help children's safety and health. Bobby Campbell, Lady Gaga's manager, opens up about how he helps one of the most significant musical and social voices of our time use her talent and fame to collaborate with brands to do more good. And Andy Fyfe, head of community at the nonprofit B Lab, gives us insights about the revolutionary B Corps, such as Kickstarter, Etsy, and Ben & Jerry's, that are creating a new corporate model for "doing well by doing good."

Laura Probst

Head of Social Goodness, the Honest Company

Too often corporate social responsibility (CSR) has become a tired exercise: photo opportunities and window dressing to show the public that a company really does care about being a good corporate citizen. But what if you could "reinvent CSR" to be a vibrant force for good, one that brings the company's purpose to life in new and unique ways? In this chapter, we meet Laura Probst, the Honest Company's head of social goodness, who is doing just that.

The Honest Company is a fascinating example of what happens when an architect of cool decides to start her own social business. Golden Globe–nominated actress Jessica Alba (star of such films as *Sin City*, *Little Fockers*, and *Fantastic Four*) had a childhood involving asthma- and allergy-related illnesses; when she became a mom herself and was washing her daughter Honor's clothes with a detergent that caused herself to break out in hives, she had a moment of awakening. She started investigating the chemicals used in products and realized that some toxins could be labeled in misleading ways.

That epiphany led her to cofound the Honest Company in 2011 with Christopher Gavigan, an expert in how the environment affects children, whose book *Healthy Child Healthy World* addressed many of the issues Alba was focused on. They were both fueled by the purpose of creating a range of safe, nontoxic baby products that avoided many of the harmful chemicals found in many other products. They wanted to create a "dream brand" that, in their own words, had "savvy style, sustainability, and extraordinary service and convenience all wrapped in a passion for social goodness, tied with a bow of integrity and sprinkled with a little cheeky fun."

They define the purpose of their company as being "to build healthier, safer families," and so far the response has been rapturous. Despite weathering storms around product ingredients, the company's sales in 2023 were $344 million and was valued at $550 million. It now serves customers in the United States, Canada, China, and Europe. The company has benefited greatly from the publicity generated by its charismatic founder. The company has spent little or nothing on traditional media such as print ads, TV, or out-of-home advertising, relying instead on the publicity generated by its charismatic founder (who has more than 6 million Instagram followers), as well as the strong word of mouth generated by its loyal fans.

In 2015 the Honest Company debuted Honest Beauty, a separate range of 83 skin-care and makeup products, with ingredients derived from botanicals and free of many of the common chemicals found in such products. Alba and her team have also lobbied Congress on multiple occasions, demanding higher standards of labeling, not just on toiletries but also on clothing and toys for children. Unlike other celebrity ventures (Gwyneth Paltrow's Goop springs to mind), part of the Honest Company's appeal is that they don't deal in rarefied celebrity aspirations but rather empathize with the day-to-day problems of all parents. And they have also tried to ensure the products remain relatively affordable and within the reach of all parents.

The Honest Company also does a tremendous amount of "Social Goodness" (their term for CSR) partnerships, focusing mainly on early child development, as well as training young people to help achieve their dreams. They partner with a tremendous range of nonprofits, including FoodCorps, the Center for Environmental Health, and Girls Who Code. In addition, they have funded things like the Honest Company Ultra Clean Room at Mount Sinai Hospital in New York City, a state-of-the-art facility that can measure the impact of chemicals in the environment on children's health, and will reduce the turnaround time for test results from 18 months to less than two weeks.

We spoke to Laura Probst, who was the head of social goodness, about how her journey started and some of the insights she gained along the way. (She's now the principal and chief strategist at her own consultancy Do Good, Make Money, helping many Fortune 500 companies with her deep experience.) "I always knew that I wanted to find a career making a difference. It was how I grew up and what motivated me. I had been working before that and really wanted to do something service-oriented; I kind of wanted to go in the Peace Corps, and that kind of scared my mom," she laughs. "Peace Corps was a two-year commitment, so I thought I'd kind of go and do my own project that I could go do for several months [as opposed to two years], and then [I'd] go off to law school."

Laura's path to purpose started when she was working with a women's empowerment organization in South Africa, helping ensure the viability of its microenterprise program through a strategic partnership with Woolworths. She says, "I did some work in South Africa with a nonprofit back in 1999. We saw that women in the program just needed to have dinner tonight. And we went up the road to a Woolworths and asked them what they did with the damaged cans and the food that was about to expire, because we needed to give our women dinner and they are dropping out of our program, and we wondered if they would consider donating it to us. And we found that this was actually quite a problem for them because they had to dispose of the expiring food, and that cost them money and resources. And they were thrilled with the idea that we might actually take their problem and turn it into something good—and make them look good—by doing some positive PR. So they gave us the opportunity to start transporting the dented food, and we saw the rates of the program go up, and the company started to ask, 'Well, what else can we do for you?'

"So for me it was a very big aha moment of, 'Oh, OK, this is a very powerful way to make a difference because you can get these huge companies which have lots of resources—actual products that I want, financial resources, talent, volunteers. So if we can just make this work for them, they're so willing to do more. And so that's really what got me on my path of creating real win-win partnerships between brands and nonprofit organizations."

In an era when many brands are claiming to do good, Laura pointed out one important fact: "I think it needs to be clear and simple. People need to very easily get it, where the money goes, and they need to relate to it, to see movement. A lot of people love the idea of doing good but can end up feeling very defeated in that journey, depending on what kind of 'doing good' you are offering them. For example, if you offer them a chance to 'do good to help cancer,' a lot of money and effort has gone into that, but we still have a very big cancer problem. If you look at things like the ALS Ice Bucket Challenge—the fact that they followed up after one year and they actually had had tangible results to show—I think that's what made it really cool."

Laura talks about how it was important to build programs that had the transparency and the accountability to show people how their contributions made a difference. She says, "People need to feel like 'I made a difference. I helped move the needle.' When they are joining in and engaging . . . you can fulfill them by allowing them to see that something real happened. 'charity: water' lets you see the wells they build. DonorsChoose: if you help a classroom, you get a thank-you note from the actual kids. [Donors] need to know that all their money didn't go into a pit."

Laura brings up an important point: in a world where people may have a sense of fatigue about all the problems demanding attention, and a sense of hopelessness about whether their individual actions can actually make any difference, it is tremendously important to show the results. We call this principle Backing Up the Promise (the cause or the big idea you are inviting in) with the Proof (showing the results of all the collective action that has taken place).

Laura also points out how this translated into the actions of brands and raised the stakes for them. "In the past brands could benefit by putting a pink ribbon on their packaging," she says. "But now consumers demand more because brands like TOMS and Warby Parker have given them simple models—buy a pair, give a pair." And people say, "I like that; it's simple. If I am really doing good, show me what good I am doing."

We move on to talk about her current role at the Honest Company. "As head of Social Goodness, I oversee all of our missions' outward and internal engagement activities, from employee volunteerism to all of our philanthropy and social giving, cash and grants and product donations. All the communications around that, creating cause-marketing programs, thought-leadership opportunities, and really leading the policy-engagement efforts that bring our social-impact mission to life. It's like the head of CSR, but we call it Social Goodness because our brand is cool and has a cheekiness to it!"

We dived deeper into what Laura means by Social Goodness in the context of the company. She tells us, "Social Goodness is at the heart of what the Honest Company is about. Jessica had a non-profit vision but created a for-profit business to make it sustainable. The goal was always social impact, and the company was the means to make it possible. We're not out there in all our communications or advertising talking about our social responsibility, but that's at the heart of who we are—and it comes across more clearly in some communications than others. We see it everywhere, from the way our customers talk about us to the lists we get included on to the thousands of employees who see us as a mission-driven brand; they want to know more about what . . . the mission [is], and they want us to define what the change is that we want in the world."

We ask Laura what she is most proud of in her time at the company, and she says, "When you start out as a start-up you don't have a lot of money to make change with. What we did have was the spirit of our employees who wanted to get out into the community and make a difference. So we really built a culture of giving inside the team. And because we had Jessica, other people wanted us to join in their campaigns. And obviously the products we are making, in everything we do, we're making responsible, healthy, safe products, which makes people feel like they are providing healthy, safe options for their family."

The sheer diversity and number of programs that the Honest Company supports is quite staggering. "We've tried a lot of things; we've been really willing to give to a lot of different programs, and it's only been in the last year that we've asked, 'What's unique that needs a lot of help, that we can really focus on and make a big difference [in]?' First, investing in environmental health research, taking what we've learned and translating that into programs and interventions that can really help in the early education space, and really trying to take some of those program impact results and trying to change policy—so that there really are standards and regulations that make health and safety more accessible to everyone.

"We started to see a lot of people like our products, and a lot of people like our education, so we started to see that we really had a bit of influence. So we started to think about how we would use those assets and those resources to do the most good. And that's when we started to look at investment, and we were starting to see problems in the world that were unsolved. So one of the investments we made was in creating the Honest [Company] Ultra Clean Room at Mt. Sinai Children's Environmental Health Center.

"Before this, scientists were needing to take lab samples for environmental health research and send them out for testing, which could take up to eighteen months. Now with the Ultra Clean Room, where they can do the testing in-house, that turnaround time has been reduced to two weeks. We've already seen some really interesting developments come out of that Clean Room. We're not funding research, but by creating the Clean Room, it attracted amazing researchers, which has started to give us things like methodologies for testing autism in kids under two years old, which didn't exist before. We see things like autism, allergies, early childhood diseases rising, and there are a lot of questions that parents are asking: 'Why is that happening? Is it genetics, is there anything else going on?' And our hope is that we can help find some answers. Does the environment have anything to do with it and, if so, what? How do we gather information so we can make choices? I'm really proud of the work we are doing with the Ultra Clean Room."

Hearing Laura talk with such passion and enthusiasm about her work makes us realize that another fascinating aspect of the story is how backing up "the Promise" with "the Proof" also works in another way. When brands get involved in a cause and use it in their marketing (like, for instance, Dove has done with its "Campaign for Real Beauty"), then if the brand does not put their money where their mouth is [by] actively engaging in partnering with organizations to take action (like Dove has done to partner with entities like the Girl Guides, Girl Scouts, and the Boys & Girls Club to help start programs around self-esteem and body confidence issues), then it is just empty rhetoric. It is exploitation of an issue for brand benefit without contributing anything in return. Customers are too savvy these days to just accept this; in the era of the Internet, it is all too easy to see exactly what companies are doing to back up their claims.

"In the last year, we have also identified another area in which we can make a difference; early education settings are a truly underfunded space. Only four percent of public funding goes into early education, but the early years of education, up to age five, are the most important for a child's development. Sixty percent of moms go back to work within six months of giving birth, which means that moms and dads need to rely on child care, and there's no standards for 'What is a healthy, safe place for my kid?' There's a lot of work being done on healthy, safe schools, but child care doesn't have access to information, to healthy, safe nutrition programs, programs on health and safety; they even have requirements on cleaning with bleach! And we'd like to see some standards created on what is a healthy, safe early child-care environment because 12.5 million kids are in a child care center, which is a hugely influential thing for them. And so far, we feel like we've been making a pretty big dent. We've donated a lot of our products to child-care centers, and we've helped over a hundred thousand children so far."

Laure clarifies that she thinks there is still a need to have marketing communication that is focused on products and their attributes. "Of course, it's a balance between efficacy, which is hugely important because nobody wants to use a product which doesn't work, and the social goodness; and we can dial up different pieces of that depending on what we talk about. But it's important that those values are clear to our customers. I think a lot of go-forward communications to our customers are going to articulate the tangible and easy things . . . that they can do. Our customers have certainly shown that they do want health and safety to be accessible to everyone, and they love that we are a brand focused on creating a movement—that means something to them."

Laura talks about the level of engagement and advocacy from their community and stakeholders. "A portion of every purchase helps fund our programs, so just by purchasing they are helping to make a difference; we message that on every product we sell. We create special opportunities for them to engage with us, whether it is a social media campaign, where if you use a hashtag you can generate funds, which we can use for a particular program. We try to have some activation opportunities for our customers to engage with us, like when we went to Capitol Hill to talk about the Toxic Substance Control Act and the reform that's being considered in Congress. And rather than put up a petition, we put up a video of Jessica and Christopher and their visit, and we saw huge engagement levels around that—three times the norm.

"If you look at how fast the company has grown, and how fast we got to 1.4 million followers on Facebook, I think we are seeing that people are hungry for these solutions and what we're offering. So I am seeing a really high level of engagement in the purpose of the brand; I want to bring health and safety to my family, and I want to bring it to my community."

This ties into something we have seen everywhere; people are hungry to get involved in something that is meaningful, something that is bigger than themselves. If brands can provide opportunities for participation, we feel that this is something way more powerful than traditional marketing; inside of being selfishly focused on getting the brand's message across, the brand can provide a platform to create a movement built around common cause, providing people with an avenue to participate. To put it another way, it's the customers themselves who can provide the "Proof" to back up the "Promise."

Why We Love This Example: The Honest Company has redefined CSR to provide that "Proof" in a living, breathing way. Instead of it being the window dressing it all too often is at major companies, a chance to deflect criticism with some well-publicized photo opportunities and charitable donations, at the Honest Company it is something deeply rooted in the purpose of the company. Not only does the Honest Company give a broad range of scalable, flexible opportunities for employees to take ownership across the country, but it also goes above and beyond in backing flagship projects such as the Ultra Clean Room, all of which help provide multiple sources of "Proof" that the company is serving its Purpose of building "healthier, safer families."

Bobby Campbell

Manager, Lady Gaga

Few artists have more successfully leveraged their artistic voice in service of their social voice than Lady Gaga. Her fearlessness in tackling some of the most controversial issues of our time has directly fueled the deep devotion that her fanbase of "Little Monsters" has for her. We talk to her manager, Bobby Campbell, about how she walks that artistic tightrope.

The lights go up at the Dolby Theatre in Hollywood, California. It is the 2016 Academy Awards and the vice president of the United States, Joe Biden, walks onstage and gives an impassioned speech about the issue of sexual abuse and the need to create a culture of consent. He then introduces Lady Gaga, who performs her Oscar-nominated song "Til It Happens to You" from the documentary film *The Hunting Ground*, which covers the issue of sexual abuse on college campuses. At a pivotal moment she is joined by 50 survivors of sexual abuse, all of whom have written messages such as "Not Your Fault" and "Unbreakable" on their arms in support of the performance. When Gaga raises her arm, you can clearly see the word "Survivor" written there too, signaling that she too has been a victim. It is a powerful, raw, vulnerable statement that very few artists in the world could have pulled off except Gaga.

It culminates an extraordinary few months in American history, in which some of the biggest artists in the world have used highly visible pop culture moments to draw attention to social issues. Beyoncé chose the Super Bowl to drop her "Formation" single and highlight the issues around police brutality, Kendrick Lamar's thrilling, visceral performance at the Grammy's proudly supported #BlackLivesMatter, and Gaga's Oscar performance closed out the trifecta (not to mention Leonardo DiCaprio also using his long-awaited Oscar win to highlight the issues around climate change). It's been a long time since major artists were this openly activist about the issues facing America, and it signals a new willingness on their part to use their spotlight to drive social change.

Of course, Stefani Germanotta, aka Lady Gaga, has always been using her platform to drive social change, ever since her inception as the fabulous, outrageous Lady Gaga. From the very beginning she has used her art and her music to challenge the status quo and speak up for the voiceless. Whether it's calling for the repeal of "Don't ask, don't tell," fighting for marriage equality, or fearlessly tweeting pictures of herself to draw attention to bulimia and body-image issues, throughout her career Lady Gaga has been as closely identified with her activism as for her art. Perhaps that is what makes her so revered by her army of fans (called Little Monsters), 83 million on Twitter/X, and 56 million each on Instagram and Facebook, all of whom follow her with a passionate intensity not seen for any other musician of her time.

One of the people who has been by Gaga's side since the beginning is her manager, Bobby Campbell. Slim and animated, he attended the annual SXSW music and tech festival in Austin, Texas, where we caught up with him, fresh off a panel talking about how brands and artists can collaborate to do more good. We sit in the garden of the Four Seasons and talk about his remarkable journey and the work he has done with Gaga to help with both her artistic and social goals.

"So I was part of her journey from the beginning, and I was fortunate to be a part of that," he says. "We put together club tours that she would go play three clubs a night; a pop club, a hip-hop club, and a gay club all over the country. And it was amazing, but for me growing up a young gay kid who didn't come out until I was in college, it wasn't just that I loved the music or the visual; I loved everything about her. I loved her as a person, but there was a deeper meaning for me, in that she is an icon for a generation that I wish I had had, you know? You know, she was out speaking at gay rallies and helping to change what would affect my personal life. How could you want to work with anyone else?"

Bobby talks about some of the challenges that come with artists who want to exercise that social responsibility. "It's interesting a lot of times when you are trying to be a champion for or use your voice for changing things, people don't always want to hear it. Sometimes people just want to be entertained and have fun, and they don't want anything surprising. I believe that she will be around, doing what she does, for the next fifty years. Without a doubt. You look at Tony Bennett and he's an American classic, but if you do the research, in the '60s he was a huge voice in the civil rights movement. And I know in my heart that [Gaga] will be around forever, and will continue to change the world over and over. And like I said before, I think she's only begun to scratch the surface. My personal mission was to get people to understand and respect the person that I know."

Gaga has always used her art to provoke society in service of a deeper message; that's what makes her more interesting than many of the more disposable pop stars in the culture today. And the emotion that she creates because of this courage is something that inspires a level of response that is spontaneous and visceral. "After the Oscars she flew the day after to Chicago," Bobby says. "And so she's in LAX, and there are grown men, grown women . . . people who would not be what you'd expect to be a Lady Gaga fan, coming up to her in tears, crying, and saying, 'Thank you. Thank you for what you've done.' And they all had some personal story connecting to the conversation on sexual assault and what that meant."

It's the way Gaga can channel grief, be vulnerable, be human. Her music doesn't make the cause great. Her causes make her music great. That's what allows her message to scale outside her gigantic fan base of Little Monsters and reach the mainstream of America. Not that this emotionally courageous approach doesn't take its toll on the artist—or unleash a storm of criticism itself. Bobby talks about some of the challenges that come with the territory.

"When you put your heart into everything you do, it all hurts," he says. "So sometimes part of the challenge is to just keep going. Despite any sort of dissent. Because when you're being a revolutionary or pioneer or actually trying to change the world, you're going to piss people off. You're going to piss people off that are fond of the status quo . . . don't want to rock the boat, right? But being able to just rise above that, to ignore it and say, 'You know what? My purpose here is much greater than maybe this person or this group can understand today. Maybe five years from now or ten years from now or thirty years from now they'll understand it better, but I've got to keep going today. And I've got to fight the fight today. Because if I don't do it, who's going to do it?'"

Bobby talks about some of the decision-making process that happens when Gaga decides to get involved in different causes. He says, "We have to figure out where her voice is strongest. She touches a lot of things—LGBT issues, sexual assault issues—but it still comes from her purpose; her purpose is things she's connected to. If it's something that's great but she doesn't have a personal connection to the story—not that it doesn't matter to her, right?—there's only so much you can do. I think once an artist does too much, it kind of just dilutes the voice. The thing with sexual assault was, it's something that she really, really, really, really feels strongly about. As someone who had experience with abuse and didn't know what to do with it at the time other than suppress it, now ten years later, she's like, 'OK, I now am in this position. I'm going to make sure what happened to me never happens to any other woman again. Or man. This is not acceptable behavior. And [we] need as a group to discuss this. And to really make people understand that this is not OK.'"

At the core of their philosophy is a simple idea. "Treating people right. You know? Because that just really extends to all of it. If you're treating someone right, something that happened to her in the studio when she was nineteen wouldn't have happened. If you're treating someone right, you're not going to be bullying someone in school. If you're treating someone right, you're not going to have a problem with whom the fuck they want to be. And so that's what we had to boil down when we were putting the Born This Way Foundation together: 'What is the mission of the foundation?' Creating a kinder, braver world . . . that's not a tangible thing. We did this launch event with Oprah at Harvard, and Gaga sat on the stage and she said, 'I am

WHEN YOU'RE BEING A
REVOLUTIONARY OR PIONEER
OR ACTUALLY TRYING TO
CHANGE THE WORLD,
YOU'RE GOING TO
PISS PEOPLE OFF.

—BOBBY CAMPBELL

trying to create a behavioral shift. I am trying to change the way people think and interact with one another.' And that's a big, lofty goal."

According to the Born This Way Foundation's website, its mission is to "create a safe place to celebrate individuality, to teach advocacy, promote civic engagement, and encourage self-expression, and to provide ways to implement solutions and impact local communities." The foundation has partnered with nonprofit community organizations such as Campus Pride, GLSEN, the National Association of School Psychologists, and Youth Service America. Bobby talks about his extremely close working relationship with the foundation. He says, "I work with the Born This Way Foundation team every single day. I help them oversee the connectivity to her, the authenticity to her, working with marketing and partnerships. It's important I stay extremely involved, because it's not a side project; it's part of her overall career."

Bobby talks about a partnership with the National Council for Behavioral Health and Viacom that was a powerful example of providing her fans with resources and help. He says, "When we did the Born This Way tour in 2013, during the US leg, we had a Born Brave bus, which was a pop-up activation from the Born This Way Foundation [that] was an actual bus that we . . . retrofitted with this interactive experience. And a 600-square-foot kind of carnival was there, and there was food and music. We tried to make it a fun tailgate, with live music and food, but then we dug a little deeper. We partnered with local organizations around the country in mental health issues, LGBT issues, body image issues—you name it—to connect youth to organizations already doing great work in their communities.

"But when the bus left at the end of the day, we didn't want to create a gap. So we partnered with local YMCAs or Trevor Project local branches to connect them to the places they might not be aware of or they might not have the courage to go to as yet for whatever reason, and try to foster relationships. And every single organization that was involved was blown away by the amount of people they reached. We had kids . . . there were grandparents bringing their four-year-old transgender grandchild who were coming . . . it was really, really phenomenal."

Bobby highlights how important it was to find partners, in both brands and nonprofits, who had a common purpose to what the artist was trying to achieve. He says, "I think there are times that it's just not for the money, it's about what is the message or the reaction you're trying to achieve. But there are times you have to find the right partner who is willing to say, 'We believe in what you're doing, we want to be part of it, and we're going to help you make it happen financially.' Over the course of two months, we engaged with 150,000 young people, in person—not just through social media. It was about creating an experience, and we couldn't have done that on our own. When you talk about providing free food, entertainment, it gets very costly very quick, so we were fortunate to have foundational partners to help fund it, and then Viacom became our media partner and helped to really augment the conversation of what we were doing but also helped find us funding for it."

Another great example is the work Lady Gaga did with Virgin Mobile around her Born This Way Ball tour. Virgin Mobile's RE*Generation program, which supports helping LGBT and at-risk homeless youth, partnered with the tour to raise funds and awareness. Fans at the shows were encouraged to text to donate money to the cause, with Gaga herself matching funds to $25,000, while fans who had donated eight hours of time to helping at-risk youth were awarded free tickets to the shows. On top of that, during each show, one lucky fan in attendance was called onstage by Gaga and told that Virgin Mobile would give $20,000 to a charity of their choice.

Other brand collaborations for good that Gaga has done include partnering with MAC Cosmetics to launch a line of lipsticks with their Viva Glam line, which has raised more than $202 million to fight HIV and AIDS. Gaga and Sir Elton John had also teamed up to launch their Love Bravery collection of clothing at Macy's, themed around the idea of inspiring kindness and living courageously. Through that collaboration, 25% of the proceeds from each piece is divided between the Born This Way and Elton John AIDS Foundations.

Bobby talks about how some of their partnerships have come about with conversations with the CSR departments, not just the marketing departments. He brings up a collaboration with Mattel, around their Monster High line of toys, based on the sons and daughters of famous monsters. It is a $1 billion franchise that includes TV specials, video games, merchandise, as well as a movie that is in the works. Gaga designed a doll that helped "inspire empowerment and acceptance among young people."

Bobby says, "The initiative that the Born This Way foundation is doing with Mattel and Monster High, that started at the CSR level. So the Born This Way foundation started a relationship with Bob Goodwin; he runs CSR across Mattel across all of their brands. And there was a courting period: we got to know Bob and the corporate culture at Mattel and what they wanted to do from a philanthropic standpoint, and he got to know what we do at the foundation. And he said, 'OK, Monster High is where we need to work. Monster High is about expressing individuality and celebrating differences,' and six months later we just announced that we're doing a doll with Monster High that Gaga is designing with her sister that will be sold, and the proceeds will benefit the foundation. So I think that meaningful things can happen from either end, and it's just really about getting everyone out at the table and seeing what the commonality is like and how you can build on th[at]."

After stealing the cultural spotlight so conclusively (performing a knockout rendition of the American national anthem at the Super Bowl, winning an Emmy for her acting in *American Horror Story*, the aforementioned Oscar performance, etc.), Gaga and Bobby look ahead to what they want to achieve next in an America that is more divided than ever before.

He says, "I'm fortunate to have grown up in a world where it's not cool to be an asshole. And seeing what's happening now with Trump and all these racists coming out of the woodwork, all over America it's frightening. And it makes me feel so disconnected from my country, in the sense that it's so different from the world that I know and have grown up in my whole life. So I definitely need to ensure that every single day I am giving back by doing some good. It's just kind of part of who I am.

"And it's funny that she and I talk about goals; yeah, it's great to have hit records and sold-out tours and stuff like that, but at the core . . . her interests are so much deeper than that, as are mine. She makes great entertainment, and great performance and great music, and I definitely want to go to her concert . . . but boy does she stand for something else in life. The legacy that will be established over time is so much bigger than how many No. 1s [she'll have] in the hall of records. And you know, that to me is ultimately the mark that she and I want to leave. And it's important; without those things you don't really have the voice to effect the change so they all work together, but to sit and dream about what the world could be like when our kids are growing up, when our grandkids are growing up, that's what gets me really excited."

Why We Love This Example: In our journey on this book, we realized many of the most successful artists of any generation are the ones blessed not just with a creative imagination but also a moral imagination—which is the ability to see the world as it should be, not as it is. Whether it is Billie Holiday singing "Strange Fruit" about the horrors of lynching in the Deep South, Harry Belafonte leading the charge on civil rights, or John Lennon and Yoko Ono staging "bed-ins" to protest the Vietnam War, they understand that their art is a means to an end. The work that Bobby is doing with Lady Gaga shows that you can exercise that moral imagination in tandem with a creative one, to have a genuine social impact that can last for generations.

Andy Fyfe

Community Development, B Lab

One of the easiest ways for people to see that the products they purchase are made in an ethical, sustainable way is by certifications—such as Fair Trade for coffee. But what if you want to find out about a company, not just a product? B Corps are for-profit companies certified by the nonprofit B Lab to meet rigorous standards of social and environmental performance, accountability, and transparency. They are an assurance that a company isn't just making a "Promise" but is also committing to providing the "Proof."

Our next profile is someone who doesn't just work on one brand but in fact a whole community of brands (more than 1,400), helping them find ways to do well by doing good. Andy Fyfe was the head of community development for B Lab, a nonprofit entity that is behind the B Corps revolution in America. He's now the senior business development manager at 60 Decibels, a tech-enabled measurement company that helps improve impact performance. We meet Andy at the modest B Lab office in Tribeca, in downtown New York. Quiet and unassuming, he projects the self-assuredness of someone who has found his purpose in life and is living it every day.

For those of you unfamiliar with what a B Corp is, here's a short primer from Andy. "B Lab, a third-party nonprofit, certifies B Corporations the same way Transfair certifies Fair Trade coffee or USGBC certifies green buildings. Certified B Corporations are a new type of corporation [that] uses the power of business to solve social and environmental problems. They work to create greater economic opportunity, strengthen local communities, and preserve our environment. Through a company's B Impact Assessment, anyone can access performance data about the social and environmental practices that stand behind their products. By doing so, good companies can shine brighter and clearer than just good marketing."

Some of the most aspirational and desirable brands in the world are now B Corps. Ben & Jerry's has long been known for its social impact and became a B Corp in 2012. Warby Parker, Etsy, and Patagonia are all B Corps, as is Jessica Alba's start-up the Honest Company, which is now valued at roughly $550 million. *Inc.* magazine called B Corps certification "the highest standard for socially responsible businesses" (Inc. 2011), while the *New York Times* has said, "B Corp provides what is lacking elsewhere: proof" (Rosenberg 2011). In fact, former president Bill Clinton stated, "You ought to look at these B Corporations. . . . We've got to get back to a society that doesn't give one class of stakeholders an inordinate advantage over others" (Clinton 2012).

B Corps are a crucial evolution for a market that is increasingly driven by conscious choices about their consumption. In fact, according to the 2023 Good Must Grow Survey, 26% of Americans were familiar with the term "B Corp" (versus only 7% in 2013). And according to the same survey, 71% of Americans felt it was important to support socially responsible brands, while 66% confirmed they had purchased do good products or services in the past year. Additionally, 42% said they planned to spend more with socially responsible companies—all record highs since the survey started running in 2013.

Andy admits an early cynicism on his part about the idea of business as a force for good. He says, "I was very, very skeptical about business in general, really seeking out authenticity and wasn't finding it in a lot of the brands and the way they were communicating it. When I realized there was a community of businesses, brands I have a lot of affinity with, which I wanted to support with my dollar, it was interesting to see that there was a nonprofit working as that backbone, the engine to corral them, verify them, help them scale.

"You see, in university I became skeptical of businesses' efforts to help humanity and our planet. I considered it all greenwashing. I wanted empowerment in their beneficiaries and enlightenment in their affluent consumers. I wanted there to be a way for us as consumers, as business owners, as investors to know exactly the impact a company is having on our environment, society, and its employees. It tied a lot of things together for me. I've been here for five years, and I love it. I always wanted to be a part of something much bigger than myself.

"What I'm seeing is people voting with their dollar for a better pair of eyeglasses, or a pair of shoes, not just with their paycheck, but a much longer investment in voting for where you want to work.

And I think that same inclination to see whether my values can be aligned with this purchase is very similar to where you want to spend your day. That's a lot of human capital—what I do from nine to five. When I come to work I don't want to leave my values at home."

When we ask Andy what has changed for him in the five years since he started working for B Lab, his answer is surprising: "I know a lot less now." He elaborates, "The more you know, the less you know. You continue to ask yourself more and more difficult questions. Particularly looking at how B Corps have evolved, we call ourselves B Lab because we are an experiment; we are a laboratory of ideas which have never been put to market. We never really anticipated these things happening as quickly as they did. We're just putting out the recipe and letting the B Corps innovate with what they want to do. The mission is to support a global movement of entrepreneurs using business as a force for good, and using the power of their business to address social and environmental problems. Our ultimate mission is a shared and durable prosperity for all."

What's even more interesting is that it is no longer limited to companies that are manufacturers, with a large carbon footprint. If the 21st century is driven by intellectual property and services, then B Corps certification has also evolved to meet these needs.

"Originally when we started, B Corps certification was a way to separate a good company from just good marketing. When you go into Whole Foods or whatever, you're seeing 'organic' or 'fair trade,' which is great, but what about the company behind the product? If you're going to buy that jacket, don't you want to know about the company behind the jacket? Now the B Corps community has evolved to include 121 industries—not just products you buy but services, hospitality, marketing, web design. All these companies are realizing that there is a way to do good and disrupt that industry. More than half the community is made up of service companies; I think that's really relevant."

There are also myriad benefits that come with being part of the B Corps community. "Think about banks; there's a lot of great locally owned CDFI [Community Development Financial Institutions Fund] banks. So through our assessment we ask, 'Who do you bank with?' So it's almost like a business-development opportunity for them to be referred to as a better alternative. A bank is not going to be 'organic' or 'fair trade'; but they are a good bank, and so they deserve to be showcased."

The assessment forces companies not only to look at themselves but at their ecosystem—who they do business with and how ethical they are. Some of the earlier and larger B Corps are now helping their fellow community members not just with advice and consulting in everything from supply chain to marketing but also with financial assistance. For instance, Patagonia has set up the $20 Million & Change fund to invest in companies that are B Corps. Strategic alliances between B Corps are also common; for instance, Method worked with a fellow B Corps called United by Blue, an apparel company that helped collect recycled plastic waste from waterways that Method then used in a line of products. In fact, Seventh Generation goes a step further and actually buys other B Corps as well.

Andy speaks passionately about the need for authenticity in marketing. "More than fifty percent of the workforce is millennials, and more than fifty percent of them want to bring purpose to their work. They see through all of those good marketing campaigns. I was at a conference where Yvon Chouinard, the founder of Patagonia, spoke. The whole room was publicly traded companies talking about their sustainability campaigns, and one of the questions to Yvon was, 'What's your advice for marketing to them and being more authentic?' And he said, 'Stop lying. Everyone here who is under the age of twenty-five, they see through what you're trying to communicate.' I looked around and saw a bunch of young people like me who felt

Chapter 9: Back Up the Promise with the Proof   243

like he was speaking for them; they were just glowing. You can see that shift in generations . . . and to see it spoken by Yvon, who is such a rebel, an accidental businessperson, was amazing."

The B Corps certification now provides an easy shortcut for companies to convey their social-good credentials. "Newer companies who don't have much time to pitch their story can now just use B Corps to encapsulate that impact; it pushes early stage companies to focus not so much on marketing but on their core story. Not many of the B Corps community went to business school or learned marketing, so it is a great shorthand that helps convey the story. Method is an example of a company that is very sleek design, in a very cluttered industry; they don't put the B Corps logo on their product (we don't require it on any brands), but it's baked in the DNA of their company. It's so much more holistic than CSR or this side-marketing campaign; it's something I really believe in for our company. Which is great because the fresh blood and young energy in the company is saying, 'Huh, maybe we could be a B Corp. Let's give them a call!'

"One of our B Corps, Free Range Studios, [has] this idea around 'making your customer your hero.' Traditional marketing in the past has made you feel like you are the victim or the enemy—'you're not pretty enough' or 'you need to buy this because it will make you better.' Now it's flipping its own on its head, and a lot of B Corps are recognizing that it's that humble approach . . . the brand stops saying it's the hero; we're not solving the world's problems. By their customers being engaged, and them supporting a civil society, they are becoming the hero. That's what really creates that brand allegiance and allows them to be your champion, your best ambassador."

Many architects of cool have also gotten involved in the B Corps movement as well. "Woody Harrelson is behind a company called Step Forward paper, which is a certified B Corp, and

Jessica Alba, of course, has the Honest Company. We have another B Corp called One World Football, an indestructible, self-inflatable soccer ball. The founder was an incredible inventor who went out and donated soccer balls to communities and came back to find it destroyed—but the kids had designed their own ball from bundled newspaper. It was like 'the power of play'—these kids are already being innovative in their own way. So they designed something which was durable and tapped into that yearning for play, particularly in places like refugee camps. The founder was friends with Sting, who said, 'I believe in this and will fund you.' Long story short, Chevrolet got into the mix and bought 1.8 million soccer balls; and now they have all these ambassadors like Landon Donovan and Brandi Chastain helping to give out these balls."

The kinds of brands that want to be B Corps have also now changed drastically since the beginning. It's gone from brands designed with purpose at their heart to a lot of major multinational brands like Unilever and Danone thinking about reverse engineering this kind of social commitment into their existence. "When I started we had a few founding B Corps that were larger like Method, but they were primarily small brands. Since then, we've seen Pom Organics being acquired by Campbell's Soup Company, Method being acquired by Ecover, and the Etsy IPO; a lot larger brands have come on board. You have Paul Polman, the CEO of Unilever, saying 'We want to be the largest B Corps.' . . . It could be a challenge for Unilever, but that would never have happened five years ago."

When asked whether he would like to see a world where 100% of companies are B Corps, Andy laughs and says, "Yes, absolutely. Our goal is to put ourselves out of work. I think that's going to take a long time. Our goal is to make sure our assessments get more and more rigorous, which will inspire companies to switch things up. Not just for consumers, but for investors, job seekers, academics. . . . Everyone is getting that discerning eye for what's under the hood."

Why We Love This Example: As of February 2024, there are 8,254 certified B Corporations across 162 industries in 96 countries. Andy and the team at B Lab are showing that in just a short period of time, an enormous amount of change can take place. They are showing that giving people a chance to identify ethical companies has exponential dividends in helping accelerate the growth of businesses that have a social impact—as well as holding those companies to backing up their word with their deeds. B Corps are the vanguard of a new type of capitalism, a ray of hope showing that business leaders are open to a new model.

Part III

How to Get Started Today

STEPS TO GET STARTED

1 FIND YOUR (INTERNAL) ALLIES

2 START WITH WHAT YOU HAVE

3 CLARITY FOLLOWS ACTIONS

4 DON'T FEAR ACCUSATIONS OF BRANDWASHING

5 RESPECT THE PROPORTIONS

6 PRACTICE THE GOLDEN RULE

7 ADD SOME GOOD TO THE BRIEF

8 SHARE YOUR WORK

9 PAY IT FORWARD

Chapter 10

Dream It, Do It, Share It!

OK. You've read all of these inspiring stories of people and their paths to purpose. Now it's your turn.

As authors, our goal is to inspire you and others to join in this movement and be better marketers and citizens by balancing profit and the needs of your customers and communities while still innovating and harnessing the force of popular culture.

It may seem daunting; it may seem like an impossible mountain to climb. But here are some small steps to get you started.

1. Find your (internal) allies: Somewhere inside your organization there is someone else who wants to use their talents and resources to do more good in the world, the same as you. Perhaps it's the veteran CSR person. Perhaps it's the new intern. Whoever they are, seek them out. Put forth your intention to help out into the universe, and you will be amazed by what comes back.

2. Start with what you have: Don't get hung up on the fact you may not have a big budget. Find a way to experiment. Start by donating products or services to an organization you identify with. Do some pro bono work to help meet new people and get out of your comfort zone. Sometimes it takes a while to figure out what inspires you. Get your feet wet and try out a variety of things to see what you identify with the most. Do a "beta test" with a tiny amount of money.

3. Clarity follows action: This is an important one. When you start, you may have no clear idea of how to best make an impact. Sometimes it takes a few tries to figure it out. The important thing is not to be paralyzed by fear. Learning is an iterative process that happens by doing. At the very least, you'll meet some nice folks along the way.

4. Don't fear accusations of brandwashing: Look, all organizations have something they can be criticized about. Critics can find ways to attack your business practices, your carbon footprint, a million different things. But that shouldn't paralyze you into inaction. It shouldn't make you feel cynical about your ability to create change. Be open and honest about your intentions, and transparent about how this small action is not intended to solve all the problems at once. And you will find that among the haters, you will also find allies in what you believe in. After all, the journey of a thousand miles begins with a single step.

5. Respect the proportions: One of the greatest pieces of advice we got was from a young entrepreneur who said, "When a brand spends $10,000 on doing some good, and then $10 million trumpeting that in an ad campaign, then something smells fishy." That's when criticisms of brandwashing are accurate, when the proportion of actual good to amplification of the message is off.

6. Practice the golden rule: Only do things that you would want to have done to you. Think about what you would like to be on the receiving end of. Follow your intuition; if something feels wrong to you, speak up.

7. Add some good to the brief: For professional marketers, designers, and creatives, the brief is the most essential part of the creative process. So vital that brand and design firm Bassett & Partners produced an entire documentary titled *Briefly* dedicated to informing and inspiring collaborators to write better briefs to lead to exceptional creative results. In the film, John Boiler, CEO of 72 and Sunny, went as far as to declare: "The role of the creative brief, I don't think has ever been as important as it is now. It is an open statement of ambition for a brand or client." So imagine the potential power of impacting a greater good becoming a core part of every brief and brand ambition. That change can help to unleash purpose-driven creativity in profound ways. As Frank Gehry said, "I don't think there is any lack of places to go creatively that wouldn't be worth exploring in the interest of humanity being better."

8. Share your work: For those of you working on interesting projects that aspire to grow sales through making a positive impact in the lives of others in cool ways, go online and post what you are working on with the hashtags #goodisthenewcool and #showyourwork. Austin Kleon, in his best seller *Show Your Work!*, speaks to the importance of sharing your work with communities of like-minded people. We are all drawing inspiration from the endeavors of others on a daily basis, so inspire us all by sharing your works-in-progress, big or small.

9. Pay it forward: Share this book with someone who could benefit from it. We wrote the book we wanted to read—something that spoke to the realities of marketers struggling to find meaning in their work. We want to help other marketers who have a desire to do more than just make people buy more stuff, and we know there are many of us out there. If you know any, please share our stories.

Our Final Thought: Think Transformational, Not Transactional

Hopefully all of these stories have inspired you as much as they have inspired us. We feel like we are only at the beginning of a better paradigm, one where courage replaces conformity, empathy replaces apathy, and hope replaces cynicism.

Cynicism, in particular, is what we would like these stories to help you battle—the weariness from hearing all of the negative narratives out there every day—meaningless political friction, corruption, and greed. Too often it feels safer to take refuge in a cocoon of meaningless trivia—the latest celebrity scandal, the divisive rhetoric of modern politics—and use that as fuel to believe that this world is past saving. We hope that in some small way, the stories of these inspiring people will help show that there is a better way of doing things. Good can keep being cool, but only if enough of us commit our time, energy, and passion to helping make this happen.

It starts with all of us understanding a deeper sense of our own Purpose, and ensuring we spend our time and talents working for organizations that have a higher order reason for existence other than solely for profit. Through a combination of this self-analysis and dialogue with other stakeholders, we can then find allies who have common cause. It requires all of us to think of people as "citizens, not consumers," and identify the opportunities that exist for us to not just advertise, but actually solve problems from the everyday to the epic. We realize that people are the new media and adding real value to their lives is the best way to turn them into your biggest advocates. We must ensure that when we design our ideas and products, that we lead with the cool and bake in the good—and make sure we always back up the promise with the proof. That's how we can ensure that we all help to optimize life for everyone on this planet.

Beyond those we profiled in this book, there are many more in this growing movement, who are successfully doing this and

254 GOOD IS THE NEW COOL GUIDE TO MEANINGFUL MARKETING

leading by example. People such as superstar Golden State Warriors basketball player Steph Curry, who personally donates mosquito nets to families in Africa via his foundation, Nothing but Nets, every time he scores a three-pointer. Others such as Lauren Bush—niece of President George W. Bush—and her fashion start-up, Feed, show that the idea of doing good through cool is nonpartisan. The wonderful jewelry start-up Maiyet that takes the work of artisans from around the world and shows them for the true luxury that they are; the dedicated folks at ReFoundry who help former convicts learn new skills such as carpentry that help them create furniture, and so many more. Every day we see new stories that bring us hope and inspiration for what the world can be if we choose to create it.

Certainly, that choice to use our moral imaginations to solve problems will be more important than ever. In the next 20 years, the human population will swell from 8 billion to nearly 10 billion people: the fastest population growth in the history of the planet. With this growth comes a choice: Do we continue to think in a transactional manner about the way our societies operate, continuing to do business as usual and ignoring the larger issues of inequality, discrimination, the environment, and other existential problems? Or do we choose to think in a transformational manner, finding new models and solutions to help ensure a fair and prosperous future for all?

To us, the answer couldn't be clearer; whether we work as business leaders, culture creators, or social entrepreneurs, we need to find new ways of working together that reject the outdated models of the past. We need to find new ways to utilize our unique talents that haven't been possible until now because of the generational, technological, and spiritual awakenings that are affecting us on a profound level.

Now it's up to you.

How will you start today?

Resources and Other Links

When writing this book, one of our biggest problems was figuring out which brands to include—there were more examples than we had room for! So we decided to capture all the stories we found inspiring at our blog at www.goodisthenewcool.org. You can find stories, links, and a whole lot more resources there. We hope you'll visit us and say hi.

Further Recommended Reading:

Delivering Happiness by Tony Hsieh
The Story of Purpose by Joey Reiman
Making Good by Billy Parish and Dev Aujla
Social Innovation, Inc. by Jason Saul
The Conscience Economy by Steven Overman
True Story by Ty Montague
Locavesting by Amy Cortese
Enchantment by Guy Kawasaki
Steal Like an Artist by Austin Kleon
Contagious by Jonah Berger
Youtility by Jay Baer
The B Corp Handbook: How to Use Business as a Force for Good by
	Ryan Honeyman
Let My People Go Surfing by Yvon Chouinard, founder of
	Patagonia
Breakthrough Nonprofit Branding by Carol Cone
A Selfish Plan to Change the World by Justin Dillon
Do Better by David Hieatt
Start with Why by Simon Sinek
Activate Brand Purpose by Scott Goodson and Chip Walker
Measure What Matters by John Doerr

References

Adobe. 2012. "The state of online advertising," http://www.adobe .com/aboutadobe/pressroom/pdfs/Adobe_State_of_Online_ Advertising_Study.pdf.

An, M. 2020. "Why People Block Ads (And What It Means for Marketers and Advertisers)." HubSpot Blog, January 14, 2020. https://blog.hubspot.com/marketing/why-people-block-ads-and-what-it-means-for-marketers-and-advertisers?

Blasberg, D. 2011. "Lady Gaga: The Interview." *HarpersBazaar.com*, April 13, 2011. http://www.harpersbazaar.com/celebrity/latest/ news/a713/lady-gaga-interview/.

Citi Bike. 2024a. https://en.wikipedia.org/wiki/Citi_Bike.

Citi Bike. 2024b. https://ride.citibikenyc.com/blog/100million.

Clinton, B. 2012. "President Clinton Talks B Corps." B Corporation YouTube channel, August 2, 2012. https://www.youtube.com/ watch?v=2h1TFaADqR8.

Cunningham, L. 2015. "The Tao of Paul Polman." *Washington Post*, May 21, 2015. https://www.washingtonpost.com/news/on-leadership/wp/2015/05/21/the-tao-of-paul-polman/.

Deloitte. 2024. "2024 Gen Z and Millennial Survey: Living and Working with Purpose in a Transforming World." https://www .deloitte.com/global/en/issues/work/genz-millennial-survey.html.

Dentsu. 2024. "Global Ad Spend Forecasts." May 2024. https:// insight.dentsu.com/ad-spend-may-2024/.

Dixon, S.J. 2024. "Average Daily Time Spent on Social Media World-wide 2012-2024." Statista, April 10, 2024. https://www.statista.com/ statistics/433871/daily-social-media-usage-worldwide/.

Horrigan, J. B., and M. Duggan. 2015. "Home Broadband 2015." Pew Research Center, December 21, 2015. https://www.pewresearch.org/internet/2015/12/21/home-broadband-2015/.

Inc. staff. 2011. "How a Business Can Change the World." *Inc.* magazine. May 2011. http://www.inc.com/magazine/20110501/how-a-business-can-change-theworld.html.

Khoros. 2023. "The Top Millennial Buying Habits and Insights for 2023." https://khoros.com/blog/millennial-buying-habits.

Marr, R. 2020. "One Million Moms Demands Oreo Boycott over 'Homosexual Agenda' Rainbow Cookies." MetroWeekly (Website), October 20, 2020. https://www.metroweekly.com/2020/10/one-million-moms-demands-oreo-boycott-over-homosexual-agenda-rainbow-cookies/.

Nielsen. 2012. "Global Trust in Advertising and Brand Messages Report." http://www.nielsen.com/us/en/insights/reports/2012/global-trust-in-advertising-andbrand-messages.html.

Perlroth, N. 2011. "Yves Béhar: The World's 7 Most Powerful People in Design." *Forbes.com*, November 2, 2011. http://www.forbes.com/sites/nicoleperlroth/2011/11/02/yves-behar-the-worlds-7-most-powerful-designers/#7cf2e67b7762.

Petrosyan, A. 2024. "Number of Internet and Social Media Users Worldwide as of July 2024." Statista, August 19, 2024. https://www.statista.com/statistics/617136/digital-population-worldwide/.

PwC. 2012. "Millennials at Work: Reshaping the Workforce." https://www.pwc.com/my/en/assets/publications/millennials-at-work.pdf.

Ramsey, D. 2009. *The Total Money Makeover: A Proven Plan for Financial Fitness* (Nashville: Thomas Nelson Pub.).

Rosenberg, T. 2011. "Ethical Businesses with a Better Bottom Line." *New York Times*, April 14, 2011. opinionator.blogs.nytimes.com/2011/04/14/ethical-businesses-with-a-better-bottom-line/?_r=0.

Scanlan, R. 2012. "Market Force Study Shows Companies Wield Comparable Social Media Influence to Friends." News release, GroundFloor Media, May 1, 2012. http://www.prweb.com/releases/socialmedia/retail/prweb9456629.htm.

Smith, S. 2014. "Vice's Shane Smith: 'Young people are angry and leaving TV in droves.'" Interview by Jon Swaine. *TheGuardian.com*, March 2, 2014. https://www.theguardian.com/media/2014/mar/02/vice-media-shane-smith-north-korea.

Snapchat. 2023. "Unlock Gen Z's Spending Power." August 15, 2023. https://forbusiness.snapchat.com/blog/unlock-gen-z-spending-power.

Terrazas, A. 2023. "Glassdoor's 2024 Workplace Trends." Glassdoor, November 15, 2023. https://www.glassdoor.com/blog/workplace-trends-2024/.

Zurich. 2022. "How Is Gen Z Changing the Workplace?" https://www.zurich.com/media/magazine/2022/how-will-gen-z-change-the-future-of-work.

ABOUT
THE AUTHORS

Afdhel Aziz and Bobby Jones are two highly experienced marketers, based in New York City. Their friendship and common passion for the idea of "giving back" led them to collaborate on this book, which they hope will inspire other marketers.

Afdhel Aziz is one of the most inspiring leaders in the global movement of business as a force for good.

A former Fortune 500 business executive, he embarked on a remarkable journey after surviving the devastating tsunami in his home country of Sri Lanka. This life-altering experience prompted him to seek a deeper purpose beyond the confines of corporate life.

In 2017, Afdhel made a pivotal decision to leave the corporate world and establish Conspiracy of Love as a B Corp certified global consultancy and proud minority-owned business.

He is now the cofounder and chief purpose officer of Conspiracy of Love, a global Purposeful Growth consultancy with blue chip clients such as Adidas, Sephora, The Gap, and many more.

As an international keynote speaker, he has inspired audiences at leading corporations such as Disney, Microsoft, JP Morgan Chase, and The Gap, as well as prestigious venues such as the United Nations, the Cannes Lions, and the Fast Company Innovation Festival.

Afdhel's prowess as an award-winning poet (*China Bay Blues*), novelist (*Strange Fruit*), and documentary film director (*The Genius of the Place*) underscores his fascination with the art and craft of storytelling.

On a personal note, he is a proud adoptive father, residing in Los Angeles with his wife, son, and an adorable beagle named Archie.

Find out more at www.afdhelaziz.com or scan this QR code.

Bobby Jones is a visionary entrepreneur, renowned speaker, and best-selling author who has helped leaders in over 150 countries harness the power of business and culture as forces for good. Fueled by a profound purpose to "feed the good" within himself, his communities, and the world, Bobby's work inspires us to explore new ideas, perspectives, and possibilities for our lives and careers.

Bobby is the cofounder of Good Is the New Cool, a creative studio dedicated to bridging the Hope Gap with stories of inspiration, innovation, and impact. Good Is the New Cool produces books, podcasts, TV shows, and the global conference series GOOD-Con, hosted in Los Angeles, London, Sydney, Toronto, and New York. Since 2016, Good Is the New Cool has sparked a worldwide movement of creators leveraging business and culture to drive bold actions that inspire social change.

Bobby's highly demanded keynotes and workshops empower audiences with road maps to find lasting fulfillment and meaning in their work, sparking a fire that transforms their lives, work, and the world for the better. He has spoken at events worldwide, including SXSW, the United Nations, the Vatican, Harvard University, and Feira Preta.

Bobby cofounded Conspiracy of Love, pioneering new eras of purposeful growth for the world's leading companies, including Adidas, Sephora, Oreo, Mondelez, Nike, and PepsiCo.

Bobby's latest venture, RIVET, is a Gen Z–focused social enterprise that partners with popular brands to fund youth-led change through consumer purchases. By bringing together brands, influencers, and NGOs, Rivet will invest over $250 million in youth-led social innovation over the next decade.

Bobby lives in Fort Greene, Brooklyn, with his wife and son. He is an endurance athlete who has completed the New York, Chicago, London, and Berlin marathons. Now, he is on an inspiring quest to complete the prestigious six World Marathon Majors, with Tokyo and Boston remaining in sight.

Find out more at www.bobbyjonesonpurpose.com or scan this QR code.

Acknowledgments

Afdhel and Bobby would like to thank agent extraordinaire Robert Guinsler, as well as the amazing team at Regan Arts: Judith, Richard, Brian, Lucas, Emily, Kathryn, Gregory, Clarke, Nancy, and everyone else who made this book possible.

Afdhel:

First and foremost I'd like to thank my amazing wife, Rukshana, for her patience and support while writing the book. I couldn't have done this without you. Thank you also to my parents, friends, and family around the world who keep me grounded and loved.

Thanks also to so many people along the way who gave freely of their wisdom, introductions, and support: Jerri Chou, Paul Woolmington, Catrin Thomas, Jules Ferree, Stephanie Kahan, Carol Cone, Joao Rozario, Jack Shea, Jeffrey Moran, Pierre Berard and everyone at Pernod Ricard, Andrew Hampp, Chris Johns, John Moore, Jeff Benjamin, Courtney Ettus, Drew Ianni, Jack Horner, Kiel Berry, Yusra Eliyas, Rikaza Izadeen, Ryan Gill, Sascha Lewis, Jesse Kirshbaum, Lori Corpuz, Rah Crawford, Dinesha Mendis, Robyn Shapiro, Ian Utile, Shiromi Pinto, Anthony Demby, and Tru Pettigrew.

Bobby:

First of all, thank you, Renee. I could not have done this without your love and partnership in this amazing journey. I could have written another book thanking all of the people who have touched my life and made this possible, especially my amazing family. There is no way I could thank everyone, but if you are in my life, you are appreciated.

There are some that I want to thank simply for being an inspiration to me along the way:

Miles; Mom and Dad; Lisa; Dickie and Jan; Christian Wright; Kamryn; Jaden; My Direct Impulse, Access, and YARDstyle Families; Tony and Kenny Mac; Tru; Dre; Jodi; Eric Dawson; Peace First; Bobbi MacKenzie: Mr. Kilgallon; Ann Christiano; Dao and Maxwell; Ant Demby; Troy; Shelby; Emma Holbrook; Gene; Kea; Kirk; Mike Tucker; Mike Riley; Bev; Ali; The GoodFellas.

Index

$20 Million & Change (Patagonia), 243
2020 Corporate Equality Index (Human
    Rights Campaign), 127

A

Accel Partners, 133, 134
Accountability
    ethical concerns, 36–37
    importance, 107
Achievement culture, 137
Action, clarity (relationship), 250
Activation opportunities, 225
Activision Blizzard, 105–109
    excellence, 109
Ad blockers, impact, 178
Ads Worth Spreading award, 116
Advertising
    profession, value ranking, 38
    technology, disruptive impact, 35–37
Afropunk, 132, 155–162
    ethos, 160
    excellence, 162
    initiation, 156
    online reach, 160–161
Afropunk Global Initiative, 161–162
Airbnb, Service Year Alliance
    (partnership), 103
Alba, Jessica, 218–219, 225, 245
Allies, finding, 46, 90, 98–99,
    102, 250
ALS Ice Bucket Challenge, 221
American Justice Summit, 204
Andreas Jose, 30
Arab Spring, 120
Architects of cool, 52, 54, 244–245
Artificial intelligence
    impact, 5–6
    rise, 36–37
Artistic visions, execution, 201
Artists
    evolution, 200
    social activity, increase, 200
    social responsibility, exercise, 229–230
Attitudinal shift, 179
Authenticity, 208
    importance, 197, 199
Authentic self, living, 199
Awareness, driving, 169

B

Back-end infrastructure, 98–99
Backing Up the Promise, 50, 221
"Back Up the Promise with the Proof," 4
B Corporations, 4, 9, 216, 246
    certification, 240
B Corps, 9, 216, 239, 245
    alliances, 243
    certification, 242, 244
    community, 242–244
    evolution, 242
    impact, 241
    innovation, 242
    movement, architects of cool
        (involvement), 244–245
    revolution, 240
    vanguard, 246
Béhar, Yves, 54, 56, 93
Behavioral change, 100–101
Behind the Hustle (career curriculum
    platform), 134
Belafonte, Harry, 203, 204, 237
Beneficiaries, empowerment, 241
Benjamin, Jeff, 38–39
Ben & Jerry's, 9, 77, 187, 216, 240
Best-in-class product, providing, 192
Be the Change, 98–99
"Better Food for More People" (Chobani
    mission/vision), 77–78
Bias, ethical concerns, 36–37
Bieber, Justin, 58, 65–66, 71–72
Bigelow, Kathryn, 180
B Lab, 216, 239–246
Black Lives Matter (#BlackLivesMatter), 190,
    203, 204, 228
Black people, homogeneity, 160
Bloomberg, Mike, 166
Bongiovi, Nina Yang, 151
Born This Way Foundation (Lady Gaga), 54,
    231, 233, 235
Boys & Girls Club, 224
Brand
    brand-building program, 169
    conscientiousness, consumer
        expectation, 44–45
    cool, leading, 48
    disruption, 9
    dream brand, creation, 218
    goodness, claim, 220–221

Index   269

Brand *(continued)*
  growth, 12
  kindness/tolerance embodiment, 79
  message, experiences, 35
  millennial/Gen Z expectations, 30–31
  mission-driven brand, 222
  money, making, 21
  participation, opportunities, 226
  partners, 122
  platform, providing, 226
  problem, 112
  proportions, respect, 251
  resources, usage, 179
Brand Purpose, 2
  absence, impact, 5–6
  awards, 3
  backlash, 4
  companies, interaction, 3
  initiation, 6
  movement, inspiration, 10–12
  spread, 4
Brandwashing
  accusations, 251
  guilt, 38
Braun, Adam, 57
Braun, Jagger, 68
Braun, Scooter, 58, 64–73
  goal, reaching, 67
  moment of truth, 67
  portfolio, diversification, 66
Briefly (documentary), 251–252
Bush, Laura, 255
Businesses
  building, 177
  business-development opportunity, 243
  case, development, 166
  community, 241
  engagement, 87
  force for good, 242
  positive impact enhancement, 33
  power, usage, 240
  shift, 10
  ventures, management, 72

C

Call of Duty Empowerment, 105–109
"Campaign for Real Beauty" (Dove), 224
Campbell, Bobby, 216, 227–237
Campus Pride, 233
Cancer Dream Team, creation, 102
Capitalism
  evolution, 42
  excesses, elimination, 6

Cause-marketing initiative, 57
Causes, investment, 3
Cause-washing, 117
Celebrity/fame, leveraging, 99–100
Center for Environmental Health, 219
Charities, grants (providing), 107
Chastain, Brandi, 245
Children, attention span, 203
Chobani, 10, 64, 75–81
  excellence, 80–81
  humanity, purpose, 80
  mission/vision, 77–78
  North Star, 78
Choices, consciousness, 200
Choose Love, 59, 190, 209–213
  achievements, 211
  celebrity support, 211
  excellence, 213
  funds, raising, 212
  global organization, current status, 210
  initiation, 210
  services, visual representations, 212
Chouinard, Yvon, 243
Citibank (Citi Bike), 10, 164–170
  launch, 168
  program, uniqueness, 170
  ridership, increase, 167–168
  upsides, 168
Citizens, treatment/attention, 46, 48
Clients, demands, 14
Climate change, effects, 5–6, 30, 44, 59, 113, 211–212
Clinton, Bill, 203, 240
Clinton Foundation, 103
Clinton, Hillary, 203
Clothes, usage, 28–29
Collective courage, culture, 137
Collective impact, 102
Communities
  building, initiation, 116
  direct services, 121
  exposure, opportunities (creation), 138
  partnership, success, 161
  positive impact, 16
Community Development Financial Institutions Fund (CDFI), 243
Companies
  average length, 33–35
  environment impact/policies, 31–32
  expansion, 84
Complementary skills, 57
Concert for Bangladesh (cool, using), 52
Conscious Capitalism, 42

Conscious consumers, activity, 26
Conscious Marketing, 42
Conspiracy of Love, 3–4, 124
  team, pride, 4
Consumers
  brand perception problems, 112
  conditioning, 138
  media consumer, habits, 173–174
Content, creation, 164
Cool
  architects, impact, 52, 54
  leading, 48
  power, harnessing, 21
  using, 52, 54
Cooper, Bradley, 98, 101
Cooper, Jocelyn, 132, 155–162
Corporate social responsibility (CSR), 44, 219,
      222, 235
  denigration, absence, 57
  department, absence, 79
  exercise/reinvention, 217
  initiative, 179
  redefining, 226
  reinvention, 216
  talents/resources, usage, 250
Corporations. *See* B Corporations
  power, recognition, 42
Cradle to Cradle movement, 54
Creativity, trust, 177
Cultural community, 180
Cultural points, 157, 159
Cultural sanitization, 135
Culture
  building, 222–223
  elimination, 136–137
  shift/change, 10, 21, 99
Culture of inclusiveness and tolerance, 162
Cummins, Ryan, 90
Curators, hiring, 174
Curry, Steph, 255
Customers, positive impact, 16
Cynicism, battle, 254

D
Das, Shanti, 196
Dawson, Eric, 15–16, 119–122
Democracy, idea, 180–181
Democratic Congressional Campaign
      Committee, 98
Designers, perception, 136
DiCaprio, Leonardo, 168, 228
Differences, appreciation, 154

Displaced people, supplies, 212
Dissent, 230–231
Diversity
  beauty, 154
  impact, 135, 145
DJ Khaled, impact, 199
Do Good, Make Money
      (consultancy), 219–220
DonorsChoose, 221
Donovan, Landon, 245
Dope (movie), 144, 151–153
Dove, "Campaign for Real Beauty," 224
Dream brand, creation, 218
Dulux, 113–118
  excellence, 117–118
  Let's Colour Project, 115–116
  paint, donation, 117
  project creation, 112

E
Education, 151
  early education settings, 224–225
  importance, 203
Edward M. Kennedy Serve America
      Act, 99
Efficacy, social goodness (balance), 225
Emergency operations, involvement, 20
Empathy
  empowerment, confluence, 30–31
  role, 180–181
Employee payout, calculation, 77
Enlightenment, empowerment, 241
Entertainment Industry Foundation, 102
Entrepreneurship, 138
Etsy, 9, 216, 240
  IPO, 245
Evans, Hugh, 58–59
Existential crisis, 33–35
Experiences, creation, 164
Experts, usage, 85–86
Exposure, impact, 135

F
Fairey, Shepard, 147
Fair Trade coffee, Transfair certification, 240
Famuyiwa, Rick, 151
Fashion brand, examination, 29
Fear, 128, 149
  absence, 251
  basis, 206
  fear of failure, 66, 73
  paralysis, 250

Index   271

F&M Schaefer Brewing Company, 157
Food
   desert, existence, 101
   products, 27–29
FoodCorps, 219
For-profit business, creation, 222
Frankl, Viktor, 71
Free America campaign (Legend),
     102–103
Free Range Studios, 244
Fyfe, Andy, 216, 239–246

G

Gaming for good, examples, 106
Gates Foundation, interaction, 179
Gavigan, Christopher, 218, 225
Gavrieli, Kfir, 190–194
Gehry, Frank, 252
Gender identities, inclusivity (celebration), 127
Generational driver, 21
Generation Z (Gen Z)
   action, appetite, 86
   baby boomers, workforce contrast, 32
   brand expectations, 30–31
   diversity/liberation, 125
   job offers, declining, 33
   numbers, spending power, 31, 120
   purpose/consumption statistics, 31–35
Girl Guides, 224
Girl Scouts, 224
Girls Who Code, 219
Giveback projects, 68
Global Ad Spend Forecasts, (Dentsu), 37
Global Citizen, power of cool
     (harnessing), 58–59
GLSEN, 233
Goldenberg, Dan, 105, 107–109
Golden rule, practice, 251
"Good and Cool" products/services, 5
GoodCon "Festivals of Good" creation, 4
Good Is the New Cool, 84
   global movement, 4
   website, checking, 26
Good Must Grow Survey, 241
Goop (Paltrow), 219
Got Your 6, 101
Gray, Elyssa, 164–170
Great Depression, 99
Great Lawn of Central Park, 59
Greenwashing, 38, 241
Grocery shopping, laptop (usage), 26–27
Gun violence, tackling, 85

H

Harrelson, Woody, 244–245
Harrison, Scott, 58
Hashtag, usage, 225
Hasso Plattner Institute of Design, 133–134
Healthy Child Healthy World (Gavigan), 218
Hill, Lauryn, 147
Hodari Coker, Cheo, 153
Holiday, Billie, 237
Honest Beauty, debut, 2319
Honest Company, 10, 216–226, 245
   programs, diversity/number, 223
     Social Goodness, 219, 222
     Ultra Clean Room, 219, 223–224, 226
Hopelessness, sense, 221
Howard University, attendance, 201
Human creativity, 177
Humanity
   brands, relationship, 187
   Upworthy, interaction, 175
Humanity for the Win (video series), 178
Human resource departments,
     creation, 140–142
Human Rights Campaign, 2020 Corporate
     Equality Index, 127
Humility, importance, 85–86
Hunting Ground, The (documentary), 228
Hurricane Sandy, impact, 167

I

i am OTHER, 132, 143–154
   excellence, 154
Inauthenticity, 208
Inclusion, impact, 135
Inclusiveness, culture, 162
Inclusivity, celebration, 127
Income inequality, 44
Individuality, 149, 151
   beauty, 144
Inner battle, emotions, 15
Inner-city neighborhoods, talent
     (presence), 140
Innovation, 59, 149
Integrity, 199
   alliances, social entrepreneur creation, 46
Internal allies, finding, 250
Internal company revenue pressures, 14
Internal self-reflection, 84
Internet
   impact, 224–225
   users, numbers, 36
Ive, Jonathan, 54

J

Jackley, Jessica, 192
Jay Z, 146, 204
Job
  defining, 69, 71
  losses, 76
  purpose, 68–69
Joe Camel, campaigns (damage), 37–38
John, Elton, 235
Johnson, Jaha, 190, 195–208
  accident, impact, 205
  conversation, change, 197
  core values, 197, 199
  eyes, openness (irony), 206
  fear, basis, 207
  paralysis, 205
  recovery, 196
Joy
  recognition/implementation, 68
  sharing, 73
Just Do It (Nike), Colin Kaepernick
  (involvement), 2

K

Kickstarter, 9, 216
King, Jr., Martin Luther, 202
Kiva, partnership, 192
Know Yuor Purpose, 64, 77
Koechley, Peter, 164, 171–181
Kotick, Bobby, 106

L

Lady Gaga, 216, 227–237
  Born This Way Foundation, 54,
    231, 233, 235
  causes, involvement, 231
  cultural spotlight, 236
  difference making, 52–54
  goals, discussion, 236
  grief, channeling, 230
LaFace, 196–197
Lamar, Kendrick, 228
Lappe, Anne, 30
Lead with the cool, 12, 48, 173, 254
Lean In campaign, 180
Legend, John, 90, 98, 102, 202
LGBTQ+ History Month,
  celebration, 127–128
Life (lives)
  evolution, 66
  focus, 207

improvement, 121
joy, 67–68
optimization, 38, 45
positivity, 69
soundtrack, music (relationship), 203
vision, 15, 48
Little Monsters (fanbase), 227, 229
Live 8, 59
Live Aid concerts, cool (usage), 52, 54
Love Bravery, launch, 235
Lunch meeting, 28–29

M

MAC Cosmetics, 235
Make-A-Wish Foundations, 71
"Make Money and Do Good by Harnessing
  the Power of Cool," 9
Malagueta Group, 116–117
Manager, role (importance), 201
Man's Search for Meaning (Frankl), 71–72
Market
  conditions, change, 45
  evolution, B Corps (impact), 241
Marketers
  access, 164
  advice, 93, 95
  challenge, 36–37
  customer champion, 42, 44
  need, 6
  positive impact, 16
Marketing
  advice, 243–244
  campaigns, 21
  career, selection, 21
  innovativeness, 21
  investments, flow, 44
  meaningfulness, crisis, 37–39
  practice, 42, 44
  Product, Price, Place, and Promotion
    (four Ps), 44
  profession, value ranking, 38
  ranking, 10
  responsibility, 37–38
Marketing-agency-of-record accounts,
  winning, 14
"Marketing with Meaning," 2
Marlboro Man, campaigns (damage), 37
Marriage equality, fight, 228–229
Maturity, meaning, 72–73
Mayden, Jason, 132–142
McDonough, William, 54
McGuiness, Peter, 64, 75, 77–80

Index   273

Meaningfulness, crisis, 37–39
Media
    company, creation, 174
    consumer, habits, 173–174
    golden age, 176–177
Me generation, 30–31
Mental health, 87
Mentorship, 107
Mercy Ships, 58
Meritocracy, 136
Millennials
    action, appetite, 86
    brand expectations, 30–31
    job offers, declining, 33
    numbers/spending power, 31
    purpose/consumption statistics, 31–35
"Millennials at Work: Reshaping the
        Workforce" report (PwC), 32
Mindset, shift, 138–139
Minority demographic, targeting, 137–138
Mission-driven brand, 222
Mission-driven organization/company, 176
Mobile video, impact, 177–178
Mondelēz International, 124, 127, 129
Monster High, toys, 235
Moral imaginations, usage, 255
Morgan, Matthew, 156
Music
    artists, influence, 201
    life soundtrack, 203
Musk, Elon (work perception), 64
Mycoskie, Blake, 85, 187

N
"Narrow and Deep," 107
National Association of School
        Psychologists, 233
National Council for Behavioral Health, 233
Naughton, Josie, 190, 209–213
Newsom, Marc, 136
Nicholson, Jim, 106
Nonprofits, impact, 57–59
Noontime Records, 197
November Yellow, 196
Nutritional wellness, 78

O
Obama, Barack Hussein, 99, 147, 157, 201
Obama, Michelle, 101, 201
Obesity, issue, 101

One-for-one model, 85
One Million Moms, social media flood, 129
One World Football, 245
Openness, 151
Open Society Foundation, interaction, 179
Operation #SewTOGETHER, 191, 193–194
Oprah, Winfrey, 231, 233
OREO, 10, 123–130
    excellence, 130
    PFLAG partnership, 127–128
Organizational cultures, redesign, 140–142
Organizational purpose/goals, dependence, 48
Organizations, start-up operation, 58
Outcome-oriented change, creation, 100

P
Packaging
    accessibility/approachability, 79–80
    pink ribbon, attachment, 221
Paltrow, Gwyneth, 219
"Parents, Families, and Friends of Lesbians and
        Gays" (PFLAG), 127–128
Pariser, Eli, 172
Parnell, Justin, 123–130
Partners, finding, 234
Partnership process, guidance, 148–149
Patagonia, 9, 28, 123, 187, 240, 243–244
    $20 Million & Change, 243
Peace Corps, 220
Peace First, 15
Peer pressure, impact, 101
Pencils of Promise, 57, 71
People
    connection, 173
    emotional manipulation, 44
    music artists, influence, 201
    new media, 48, 50
Pepsi (Kendall Jenner campaign), 2
Perception-shift study, 101–102
Personal protective equipment (PPE),
        obtaining, 193
Pettigrew, Tru, 14–15
Philanthropic work, 72
Playfulness, impact, 125
Polman, Paul, 33–35
Pom Organics, 245
Popular culture, shift, 9–10
Porter, Michael, 42
Power of Cool
    Global Citizen harnessing, 58–59
    harnessing, 45–50

Power of play, 245
Pride, impact, 207
Privacy
    ethical concerns, 36–37
    issues, 36
Problems
    attention, 221
    solving, 48
Probst, Laura, 216–226
Procrastination, impact, 14–15
Product, Price, Place, and Promotion
    (four Ps), 44
(PRODUCT)RED, 26, 52, 90–91
    excellence, 95
    genius, 92
    leading with cool, 92–93
Products/services, development, 6
Profitability, priority, 86
Profits, optimization, 38
Promises, backing up, 50, 221
Pronoun, selection, 126
Propper, Greg (Propper Daley), 90,
    97–101
    excellence, 103
#ProudPlatform platform, 127–128
PSAs, impact, 97
Purpose
    disruptor brands, emergence, 5
    finding, 90
    knowledge, 46
    path, 220
    priority, 86
    renewed sense, 196
    sense, depth, 254
    theme, 71
    truth, 127
Purpose-based marketing experiences/
    services, 50
Purpose-driven companies, apologies
    (absence), 86
Purpose-driven leaders, 80
Purpose-washing, 117

R
Ramsey, Dave, 31
Reality TV, impact, 199
Real-time data, audience feedback
    (interaction), 177
RED. *See* (PRODUCT)RED
Rede Autoestima-se, 121–122
ReFoundry, 255

Refugees, supplies, 212
RE*-Generation program
    (Virgin Mobile), 234
Reid, L.A., 157, 197, 208
REI, Opt Outside campaign, 184
Return on Purpose (ROP), 117
Revenue, increase, 93
Rewire America, 172
"Rise of the Cultural Alchemist, The"
    (Mayden), 140
RIVET, 59, 119–122
    excellence, 122
    Funko, partnership, 121
Romano, Fernanda, 112–118
Rose, Christina, 119–120

S
Saltwater Brewing, 185, 187–188
SB Projects, 65, 66, 68–69
Script, completion, 207
Self-critique, 174
Service Year Alliance, 103
Seventh Generation, 243
sexual abuse, issue, 228
Shared-equity platform, creation, 77
Shared struggle, glocal sense (creation), 31
"Share Your Pronouns With Pride," 126
Smith, Amy, 64, 83–87
Social activity, increase, 200
Social change
    creation, 99–100
    engagement, 196
    field, default, 100–101
Social consciousness, balance, 132
Social Goodness, 219, 222
Social goodness, efficacy (balance), 225
Social impact, 52, 54, 246
    agency, function, 98
    embedding, 192
    goal, 222
Socially responsible brands, support, 241
Social media
    channels, motivation source, 193
    platforms, 30–31, 36
    rise/concerns, 36
Social progress, championing/celebration, 124
Social responsibility, exercise, 229–230
Social wellness, 78
Societal change, igniting, 46
Society (provocation), art (usage), 230
SolarCity, 64

Index   275

SpaceX, 64
Spiritual driver, 21
Spouse employment, 107
Sri Lanka, natural disaster, 20
Stand Up to Cancer campaign, 102
Start-up, initiation, 222–223
Statement of purpose, writing, 15
Statement of Work (SOW), 187
Step Forward (Harrelson), 244–245
Storytelling, 175–176
Story, testimony (sharing), 16
Stress, impact, 101
Suicide, confrontation, 175
Surface aesthetics, 54
Survivor guilt, diagnosis, 20

T
Talent
    presence, 140
    usage, 250
Technological driver, 21
Technology, disruptive impact,
        35–37
Tesla, 9, 26, 48, 64
Thousand Oaks shooting, 85
Thunberg, Greta, 120
Tieks, 190–194
Toiletries, purchase, 29
Tolerance, culture, 162
TOMS, 9, 10, 64, 83–87, 187, 221
    excellence, 87
Toxic Substance Control Act, 225
Travel, benefit, 200
Trevor Project, 233–234
Trust gap, solving, 45–46
Turnaround time, 219
Twain, Mark, 18, 20

U
Ultra Clean Room (Honest Company), 219,
        223–224, 226
Ulukaya, Hamdi, 76
United by Blue, 243
Universal wellness, adoption, 78
Upworthy, 164, 171–181
    excellence, 171
    mission, 181
Urgency, sense (strengthening), 206
Usher, 190, 195–208
US unemployment rate, 108

V
Valdés, Mimi, 132, 143–154
    intuitions, 149–150
Validation, 5
Vega, Marco, 54, 164, 183–188
Viacom, 233
Violence, concern, 202
Virgin Mobile, RE*-Generation program, 234
Virgo instincts, 146
VisionSpring, donation, 8–9
Viva Glam, 235

W
Warby Parker, 57, 221, 240
    examination, 8
    purchases, 48
    success, 8–9
Wardrobe, products, 27–28
We Are from LA, 150
We Believers, 54, 164, 183–188
    excellence, 188
    philosophy, difference, 185
    plastic waste problem, solution, 184–185
Weed, Keith, 184
We Feed People (documentary), 30
We generation, 30–31
Whitaker, Forest, 151
Whole Foods, 242
Whole World Water campaign, 93
"Why Business Can Be Good at Solving
        Social Problems" (Porter), 42
Williams, Pharrell, 143–154
    N*E*R*D, collaboration, 147
Willig, Jennifer, 90–92, 94
Willis, Bruce, 168
Wolves, types, 15–16
Women, empowerment, 220
Word-of-mouth, creation, 9
Work
    applications, 12
    sharing, 252
    stress, 14
Worldview, enlightenment, 57
WRTHY, 92

Y
Yousafzai, Malala, 120
Youth marketing, work, 16
Youth Service America, 233

OTHER BOOKS FROM
AFDHEL AZIZ AND BOBBY JONES

GOOD IS THE NEW COOL GUIDE TO

PERSONAL PURPOSE

DESIGNING A MEANINGFUL AND PROSPEROUS CAREER

AFDHEL AZIZ & BOBBY JONES

Good is the New Cool Guide to Personal Purpose •
ISBN: 978-1-394-27486-4

GOOD IS THE NEW COOL GUIDE TO

CONSCIOUS BUSINESS

HOW COMPANIES CAN DRIVE GROWTH THROUGH POSITIVE IMPACT

AFDHEL AZIZ & BOBBY JONES

Good is the New Cool Guide to Conscious Business •
ISBN: 978-1-394-28447-4

WILEY